THIS BOOK BELONGS TO

....

CAKES
BY MELISSA

CAKES
BY MELISSA

·······································

LIFE IS WHAT YOU BAKE IT

120+ Recipes for Cakes, Icings, Fillings, and Toppings for
Endless Flavor Combinations from the Creative Force Behind

Baked by Melissa

MELISSA BEN-ISHAY

PHOTOGRAPHY BY ASHLEY SEARS

WM
WILLIAM MORROW
An Imprint of HarperCollinsPublishers

FIRST EDITION

Designed by Suet Yee Chong
Photography by Ashley Sears

Library of Congress Cataloging-in-Publication Data
has been applied for.

ISBN 978-0-06-268127-0

17 18 19 20 21   QG   10 9 8 7 6 5 4 3 2 1

FOR SCOTTIE.

You can do anything . . .

CONTENTS

INTRODUCTION

You're Amazing and You Can Do Anything 1

The Baked by Melissa Story 9

LET'S GET CAKED

What to Have on Hand 19

Melissa's Tips for Easy, Delicious Baking 26

Batters 33

Icings and Fillings 157

Glazes 215

Toppings 239

Ultimate Flavor Combos (Yum!) 265

Acknowledgments 280

Universal Conversion Chart 283

Index 285

You're Amazing and You Can Do Anything

When I was in elementary school, my father would drive me to school. It wasn't a long drive, maybe five minutes, but every day in the car he would give me the same speech: "You're amazing, you can do anything that you set your mind to, today is going to be the best day." Every day, word for word, the same speech. As I got older, I would mouth the words along with him and always say, "Oh *Dad*, come *on!*"

Both of my parents encouraged my brother, Brian, and me in every thing we did. If I scribbled on a piece of paper, my mother would say, "Oh my god, it's so beautiful!" That's just the type of parents they were—they always surrounded me with love, motivation, and confidence. It's so important to have that unconditional support in life—and in baking.

In fact, I was just as empowered in the kitchen as I was in all other aspects of life. I get asked all the time whether I had an Easy-Bake Oven as a child. I did not. Why would I have an Easy-Bake Oven when I was allowed to use the *real* oven?

My grandmothers provided my earliest inspiration and motivation when it came to cooking and baking. My grandma Annie, my dad's mom, was an amazing cook and baker. She always made it look so easy. (You'll find the recipe for her chocolate cake on page 89.) My mom's mom, Sylvia, cooked all the time, although she wasn't necessarily the best at it. That didn't matter. She was the most loving human

I've ever met and on weekends, when we visited her vacation bungalow in the Catskills, she let me make the salad. I may have been only four or five years old, but she let me use a knife. It's not *always* about sweets for me—even today, one of my favorite things to make is a really good

salad. I find the chopping very therapeutic and think of my grandma Sylvia every time.

My mom, like her mother, let me take charge in the kitchen. When I was growing up in northern New Jersey, we sat down together as a family for dinner every single night of the week—especially on Friday nights for Shabbat. The dessert was just as important as the dinner. I started baking by my mother's side at a very young age. My father is a very creative baker, and we baked together all the time as well. But Mom would let me do it all—crack the eggs, mix everything together—even though I was so small I had to stand on a chair to reach the counter. That's empowerment, and she, more than anyone, empowered me just as Grandma Sylvia did for her.

With this book, I want to empower you the way my family has empowered me. It's set up a little differently from other cookbooks: In Let's Get Caked, you'll find loads of inspirational photos of finished cakes in all shapes and sizes and lots of different flavor combinations—with complete instructions on how to concoct them. These are sprinkled among more than a hundred recipes that give you all the information you need to create these cakes—and more. It's up to you to mix and match the cake batters, fillings, icings, and toppings to create the finished cake you want. You'll find more than a hundred suggested combinations starting on page 266, but I want you to think of the recipes as your crayon box—and I encourage you to color outside the lines.

• •

I love cake. I have always loved cake. I get my sweet tooth from my dad, and as a kid, I loved dessert and snacks more than anything. I'd always have a snack when I came home from school and it often involved Oreo cookies. I'd take a glass of milk, put the Oreos in the milk, and anchor them down with my spoon—then I'd wait just the right amount of time for them to get soggy and delicious and eat them with the spoon. As I got older I learned that if you microwaved the milk—*oh my god*—that was even better! Oreos, Chips Ahoy! cookies, and

Entenmann's were what I lived on as a kid. There's nothing better than those chewy little Entenmann's chocolate chip cookies! I still could eat the whole box.

Today, the best part of my job is thinking up flavor combinations—concoctions, as I like to call them, are where my genius lies. I'm not a culinary expert—and I did not go to culinary school—but I know what I love to eat and apparently I know what other people love to eat, too. I can easily trace the variety of Baked by Melissa flavor and ingredient combinations back to my days in high school. We would go to my best friend Jen's house after school (her dad owns a kosher supermarket and a bunch of bagel stores, so they always had the best food) and I would make up all these crazy combos. Jen recently posted a photo on Facebook from 2005 and it's me, eating a bagel topped with peanut butter, Fluff, Nutella, and maple syrup. This is what we did at the end of pretty much every day of high school—we'd come home and relax, and then I'd concoct the most delicious munchies.

I see baking as arts and crafts, but you get to eat your project. I used to make scrapbooks and decorate picture frames for my friends. I love to create gifts and I think that's where baking fits in for me. In high school, I began to realize that creating and baking for people brought me a lot of joy. It made everyone so happy that I baked as often as I could.

· ·

I went to Syracuse University because my brother went there, and I followed him everywhere. Syracuse is in upstate New York, where it's very cold, so I'd choose a comfy couch over barhopping any night of the week. Sweets go a long way in satisfying the munchies, and college is where I started baking a lot: magical brownies for my friends, layer cakes with candy inside, and cupcakes—lots of cupcakes.

When I was in college, I didn't know what I wanted to do with my life, but I knew I wanted to be a mom someday, so I majored in child and family studies. I'm not a school person; I never knew how to study well and I'm lucky that I was smart enough to get good grades and pass every test. I was very chill about it: I wanted to enjoy college, and I knew I could figure it all out once I finished school. So when I graduated, I went on as many interviews as I could. I saw it as an opportunity to meet people in different positions, check out a variety of offices, and see what the environments were like. But getting a job was a priority—I wanted to earn money and move to Manhattan. That was my dream.

I went to work as a sales assistant, doing data entry at Telerep, a media sales company. It was not an inspiring job, but it got me to Manhattan and brought me a great friend—and led me to invent the tie-dye cupcake.

Michael was a salesperson who had the office next to my desk. He loved the Grateful Dead and the same kind of classic rock music that I did—we always talked about music and hippie stuff. The day before his thirtieth birthday, I asked what he would be doing to celebrate and he said, "I don't know; listening to music I guess." I wanted to do something special for him, so I decided to bake him Grateful Dead cupcakes. They were the first batch of tie-dye cupcakes I ever made—red, white, and blue tie-dye cake with the Grateful Dead skeleton face piped on top in icing. I vividly remember bringing those cupcakes into work the next morning, walking down the row of desks in this big office, and seeing everyone's face light up. Everyone wanted one and I felt bad that I hadn't made enough. At the same time, there was so much joy; the energy they provoked was like an out-of-body experience. I still get that feeling anytime I create things for people.

I stayed at Telerep for seven months before moving on to Deutsch Inc. as a media planner. It was a huge office with a casual and fun environment (employees rode scooters), and that was exciting for me. The job was cooler than my previous gig, but the work itself was still uninspiring. By this time, I was baking a ton. If it was your birthday and I loved you (and I love a *lot* of people), I baked you tie-dye cupcakes. I became known for them and, like anything that you bake again and again, I perfected them. They were beautiful, delicious, and vibrant in color. Still, when one of my friends suggested I quit my job and open a bakery, I was like, "Yeah, right, that's never going to happen."

Even though I grew up in a family of entrepreneurs, I never saw baking as a possibility for a livelihood. My grandfather founded the company that my father and uncle still run, and my brother launched an interactive web design agency with a longtime friend—but starting a business like they had didn't seem realistic. For one thing, I didn't have any experience working in food. Yes, my parents always told me that I could do anything I set my mind to, but this just wasn't something I understood as an opportunity.

And then I was fired.

Once again, it was my family who encouraged me. That very afternoon, my brother told me to go home and bake cupcakes. He said we'd start a business together—and we did. His enthusiasm enabled me to go home and bake instead of going home to sulk. I did something to make myself feel better because I know that I'm responsible for the way I feel.

That was eight years ago, and I've been working with cake every single day since. My role in the company has evolved from taking orders, baking, folding boxes, and making deliveries to running a company with multiple retail locations across Manhattan and shipping my baked goods nationwide. But my most important role continues to be flavor development. I'm constantly inventing concoctions—just like when I was back in high school. I've created hundreds of flavors over the years, and I love the challenge of finding new combinations.

I find inspiration everywhere—anytime I taste something new that I love, my first thought is how I can turn it into a cupcake. I love hot chocolate, so I thought it should be a cake. Cheesecake spread on a sugar cookie? I would totally do that. Red velvet cake with chocolate icing? Who doesn't love that?

I want people to have an experience—it's not just about cake, it's about making someone feel loved and warm inside. Sometimes I create new flavors, but I also like to take you back to childhood and re-create tastes that made you happy when you were growing up. That's the experience of Baked by Melissa, and that's the experience you can create for your family and friends.

This book is my encouragement to you. Learn one recipe and the possibilities are endless. You'll find that changing a single ingredient in a recipe can lead to whole new adventures. I want you to be as fearless in the kitchen as you should be in life. Many of the most amazing things I've done in the kitchen came about because I was trying to cover up mistakes. Maybe I wouldn't have put a glaze on top of a cake if I hadn't burned it, and maybe I wouldn't have gone home and baked cupcakes if I hadn't gotten fired. You have to take something that is a challenge and use the experience to make it better. I see challenges as opportunities—and I want you to do the same.

There was a time when Baked by Melissa was my only baby. Today I have a husband named Adi, who works with me, and we have a daughter, Scottie. In the coming years, when I drop Scottie off at school, I'm going to tell her that she can do anything she sets her mind to, that she's beautiful and amazing, she's smart and capable, and the world is her oyster.

With cake, as in life, if you believe it, have confidence in yourself, and work your ass off, you can do anything.

Melissa Ben-Ishay

Among family and friends, I'm as well known for my scrapbooks as I am for my cupcakes. I made a scrapbook telling the story of Baked by Melissa. It's amazing. I keep it here in the office and when we bring new people onto the Baked by Melissa team, I show it to them. I'm so proud of it. It took a long time to put together, but I love the process of cutting and pasting. To me, memories, love, and friendship are much more meaningful than anything you can buy.

THE
BAKED BY MELISSA
STORY

· ·

I was working as an assistant media planner at Deutsch Inc. and I wasn't good at my job. My mom gets mad at me when I say that, but the truth is, I didn't know what the company expected of me. At the time, my goal in life was to find something that I was passionate about and would leave me exhausted from hard work at the end of the day instead of seeking that fulfillment in other places. I wasn't passionate about that job, and I guess it was clear to the people at the company.

It was 11:00 a.m. on a Wednesday. I was called over the loudspeaker to the HR department. I thought I was getting a raise or a promotion, but I was fired. They told me to go back to my cubicle and pack up my belongings and thank you very much. So I went back to my cubicle and I thought, "I don't need any of this stuff." Instead of packing up I called my big brother, who is my best friend, and, crying, said, "I was fired!" Without hesitating he replied, "Don't worry, it's the best thing that could ever happen to you. Come to my office."

He and a friend, Matt Baer, had just started their own interactive agency, building websites for people, and had literally opened their office that week. I grabbed the Rolodex from my desk, thinking they could use my contacts, got in a taxi, and headed across town.

After I finished crying, we talked about what I should do. That's when Brian famously said, "I've got it. Go home and bake your cupcakes; we'll start a business out of it." This didn't come completely from left field: by this time, I had become known for my tie-dye cupcakes (I'd baked hundreds in the two years since that first batch), and we had always wanted to go into business together. When we were growing up, the conversation around the dinner table was about business and golf—my family's interests. I hated it at the time, but as I got older I realized it made me who I was and gave me a passion I'd never felt working for others. On family vacations, Brian and I would think up new business ideas; then we'd come home and actually try to implement them. So technically, this wasn't the first time that we'd tried to start a business together.

Brian told me I couldn't start a business with one prototype cupcake. "Go home and think of three other flavors," he said. "Bake them and come back tomorrow."

I left his office and stopped at the Food Emporium in my Murray Hill neighborhood, trolling the aisles for inspiration. That's when I thought up the other three flavors: s'mores, cookie dough, and peanut butter cup. Three of my favorite things in the world. I went home and baked four batches—about 240 cupcakes. They were mini, but not as small as the bite-size cupcakes we make today.

At the time, I was sharing my apartment with two childhood friends and my best friend's sister, Carly, who was staying with me for the summer while she had an internship at Alison Brod Marketing and Communications, a well-known PR firm. Alison Brod was someone I had always looked up to: she's a celebrity, she's a woman, and she's an entrepreneur. I thought it was so cool that Carly was working there, so I told her, "You know what, Carly, bring some cupcakes into work with you tomorrow. If nothing else, you'll make some new friends, because all girls love cupcakes." (I knew that the agency was all-female and that they all wore heels every day, so I was like, perfect.) In the back of my mind, I was hoping that Alison would try my cupcakes, but I didn't even know if she was there every day. She was like a myth—a legend.

Sure enough, the morning after I was fired, Carly brings the cupcakes into work and at 9:00 a.m. she's BBMing me (remember when BlackBerrys were a thing?): "Oh my god, everyone's tasting your cupcakes—and Alison Brod ate two!" Oh my god—the story could have ended there and I'd have been happy. But an hour or two later, I got another message from Carly saying, "Alison wants to put you in touch with her caterer!" Soon after that I got a phone call from a man with a thick Israeli accent: "Hello, *Meleesa*, this is Ben Zion, Alison's caterer. I would like to bring you to my house for a tasting."

Holy shit, we've been in business one day and have a tasting with Alison Brod's caterer! I couldn't believe it! I hung up the phone, grabbed my stuff, and raced to my brother's office. Mind you, this was July 1 and it was hot as hell, but I ran across town and burst into the office all out of breath and said, "You guys, we have a tasting with Alison Brod's caterer! I have to go in there like we have a business already and he could be a part of it; otherwise there's nothing that can come from this opportunity."

We needed a name and a logo. I really wanted the company to be called just Baked (a natural extension of myself), but my brother insisted that it have a personal touch. "Why do you love Alison Brod so much?" he said. "You wouldn't even know she existed if her name wasn't the name of her company." We settled on Baked by Melissa.

Matt (did I mention he's a creative genius?) was twiddling around on his computer; within minutes he turned his monitor around and asked, "What do you think of this?" It was the exact same logo that we have today. I think I teared up when I saw it—it was absolutely beautiful.

I went to the meeting with boxes that I got from the deli across the street from my apartment. Matt mocked up the boxes and pasted labels with the logo on top. I decided to make mini cupcakes without paper, so the aesthetic was just like they are today, very simply designed with a little touch of the filling on top so that you could tell the flavor of the cake. Ben took a bite of each one and he loved them all. At some point, it was suggested that I make them even smaller, so that each cupcake would be just one bite.

I left the tasting with the realization that I had a chance to do what I love every day—all I needed to do was find a way to make those cupcakes just one bite. I was so naïve, I didn't even know such a thing as a baking supply store existed. But I found a temporary solution, baked a batch of single-bite cupcakes, and brought them back to Ben. "Great," he said. "I have an event next week at the Havaianas Showroom on Spring Street in Soho. Make me 250 cupcakes and come in a black dress. Bye!" I had to go out and buy the dress (and yes, I still have it).

I showed up at the event having no idea what to expect, but Ben had purchased this gorgeous clear acrylic jewelry box to display the cupcakes, and they looked beautiful. Matt had designed business cards with my name, my cell phone number, and my home address. (Of course, nobody knew that, but my parents were *not* thrilled.) We placed the business cards in front of the cupcakes. Brian and Matt had also set up a beautiful Baked by Melissa website. The three of us actually shot all of the photographs for it in my apartment living room, with the cupcakes sitting on a white sheet that covered the coffee table, using a Canon point-and-shoot camera. Through the website, you could order a hundred cupcakes or more and pay through PayPal; I would bake them, box them, and deliver them from my apartment.

People at the event that day freaked out over the cupcakes. They grabbed business cards and that's how we started getting orders. On days when I didn't have a lot of orders to fill, I would also cold call other caterers. "Hi! This is Melissa from Baked by Melissa. I'd like to bring you a free tasting of my cupcakes." Honestly, I felt like a fraud when I was making those calls, but I got a lot of business that way, too.

We had no funding, and I had no savings. Luckily, starting up didn't cost very much, as we were able to draw on all three of our talents. Every time a company or an individual placed an order, I would get paid and turn around and buy more supplies to make more cupcakes.

My most fateful tasting was at Café Bari, on the corner of Broadway and Spring Street. Mind you, Soho was very trendy, and I walked in wearing my Syracuse sweatpants, which were splattered with batter and flour. So I was pretty intimidated when this handsome guy, Danny Omari, the owner, walked down the stairs. He took a cupcake, popped it in his mouth, looked at me, and said, "I love you and I'm storing you in my phone as Cupcake. I'll be in touch."

A few weeks later I got a call: "Hi, Cupcake, this is Danny from Café Bari. I have an idea—let me know what you think. Every holiday season I take a booth at the Holiday Market at Union Square. I usually sell soup and hot cocoa and it does okay, but I think your cupcakes could make a killing. What if you move into some extra space I have here in my kitchen in Soho at Café Bari, bake them here, and sell them to me at cost. I'll brand the booth Baked by Melissa and sell them from the booth at the holiday market instead of the soup and hot cocoa and we'll see what happens."

We met with him and decided to go forward. I distinctly remember feeling completely overwhelmed when I saw the huge kitchen at Café Bari. I was still doing all my baking in my little kitchen in Murray Hill—the same one I shared with two roommates. Waiting for the 6 train on my way home, I started crying. I was standing on the sub-

way platform thinking that I didn't want people to feel bad for me, but I didn't even know if I was excited or scared. That's all part of being an entrepreneur—you have to take risks and you have to take yourself outside your comfort zone, because if you don't go after new experiences then you won't move forward. And moving into that kitchen was going to be a huge challenge.

On November 28, 2008, seven months after I was fired, my dad drove in from Jersey and helped me move all my baking stuff to the Café Bari kitchen. We hired our first employee and the two of us baked sixteen hours a day, seven days a week for the six weeks that the Holiday Market was open. We would bake-bake-bake and Danny would come and take everything we made. We sold out every day and were so successful that we decided to open booths at the sister Holiday Markets in Columbus Circle and Bryant Park before the season was over.

When the Holiday Markets ended on January 1, we realized that we had to take advantage of this unbelievable opportunity. We decided to open our very first retail operation and in true Baked by Melissa fashion, it was a bite-size pick-up window that was attached to Café Bari.

It took some time, but we opened on March 5, 2009. I was so exhausted that first day that we hired somebody else to work the window. I had baked enough cupcakes and was sitting at the bar just prior to opening. I was freaking out—who's going to stop at this hole in the wall and buy cupcakes from someone they've never heard of before?—and didn't appreciate the banter between the bartender and the man sitting next to me. That man turned out to be David Z, another entrepreneur, a regular coffee drinker at Café Bari, and well known throughout Manhattan as the owner of a chain of fashionable shoe stores. David's quite a character. He looked at me and then at the bartender (whom I also had never met) and asked, "Who is this beautiful girl?" The bartender looked me up and down and replied, "That's my wife." "What a jerk!" I thought to myself. Turns out he was right—and that's how I met my husband.

The night before that first (and fateful!) day, Baked

by Melissa was fortunate to be written up by *DailyCandy*, one of the first online newsletters. They included us in their weekend guide the night before we actually opened our doors. That morning, we had a line that wound around the corner on Spring Street.

During that initial period, my parents came into the city every Saturday to help out. My mom would sit in the corner and make boxes while I was baking, and my dad would run cupcakes up the stairs from the kitchen to the booth. All of us, as a family, we couldn't believe it. It was crazy and it was magical. I mean, I love cupcakes and I loved to make them for my friends—but now we have Baked by Melissa and people are lining up around the block to buy them? It was insane. And it was awesome.

My brother, Brian, was the CEO. Matt designed everything, from the website to the signage to the stores. Ben Zion is a PR genius—if someone tells him no, he is going to make it a yes. He got our cupcakes backstage at concerts, behind the scenes on movie sets, and everywhere in Manhattan nightlife. Danny Omari not only gave us our first store and our first commercial baking space, but he also helped build out the stores. The five of us founded Baked by Melissa and we were a team. But we wouldn't have succeeded if those cupcakes didn't taste amazing—you need an unbelievable product to start something great.

The bartender who became my husband was also working in real estate at the time, but after three months he quit bartending to work for us, making deliveries. We needed the help! Now he and I work side-by-side in product development and he takes everything that I create to production. He's my secret weapon.

So when people ask me how I did it or call me a genius, I tell them, I didn't do it myself. Baked by Melissa is a collaboration. You can't do something like this alone: you have to recognize what you're great at and surround yourself with people who have the strengths that you don't. That's exactly what we did at Baked by Melissa, and that's the magic behind where we are today.

Baked by Melissa was a combination of preparation meeting opportunity. We were prepared. My brother and I had always wanted to start a business together. Baking cupcakes for a living? That would be my dream come true, and when I knew that I had the opportunity to do what I loved every day, I was going to do everything that I possibly could to make that happen. Because if I didn't try, I knew that one day I would look back and wonder what might have been, and I couldn't live my life that way. I never want to think coulda, woulda, shoulda. You *have* to do everything you possibly can to achieve your goals, and it's that mind-set, paired with hard work and collaboration, that brought us to where we are today.

Now we have multiple locations and ship our baked goods nationwide. In addition to cupcakes, we make bite-size, double-stuffed macarons and muffins.

In 2016, Brian—ever the entrepreneur—was ready to move on to new ventures. After eight years as CEO, he was stepping down (although he remains on the board). Brian led the search for our new CEO, someone who could lead the company to its next level in a positive way. When we met Seth Horowitz, we knew he was magic.

In September, he joined Baked by Melissa. He is wise and positive and brings a skill set and experience we've never had before. Hiring a new leader for an exciting new phase for Baked by Melissa was seamless and magical, a change that could be daunting for so many businesses. Together, we make life sweeter for people all across the country, and there is so much more to come.

WHAT TO HAVE ON HAND

BASIC BAKING EQUIPMENT AND OTHER HANDY TOOLS

You don't need special equipment to make any of the baked goods in this book, but there are some things that will make the baking—or the cleanup—easier. Feel free to improvise. If you don't have an offset spatula or a bench scraper, use the edge of a metal ruler. I like disposable pastry bags, but a plastic bag with a corner snipped off will work for icings and decorating too.

ELECTRIC STAND MIXER. A KitchenAid or similar model, with whisk and paddle attachments, makes mixing batters and icings easy, but you can also use an electric hand mixer or even a bowl and a wooden spoon or hand whisk.

FOOD PROCESSOR. The best wedding gift ever. Even a small food processor (or high-powered blender) is useful for chopping nuts, blending fresh mint with sugar (see page 155), and making crumbles (see page 242).

BOWLS. In addition to mixing bowls, I like to have a lot of bowls in different sizes for everything from simply holding ingredients, to separating batters and icing that will be dyed different colors, to melting chocolate or peanut butter. Have a mix of stainless steel and microwave-safe glass.

MEASURING CUPS AND SPOONS. In addition to a standard set of dry measuring cups and spoons, a glass liquid measuring cup is good to have on hand. It's easier to measure and pour liquids and it can go in the microwave.

RUBBER SPATULAS. For stirring and scraping (and tasting).

CAKE PANS. One of my missions with this book is to show you that the cakes can be made in any type of pan, so you don't have to go crazy at the cake supply store (unless you want to). You can even bake these cakes in a waffle iron (see page 29). The pans used in this book are:

Half-sheet pan (13 x 18 inches)
Quarter-sheet pan (9 x 13 inches)
9-inch round cake pans

THE GENIUS OF THE SHEET PAN

Many of the layer cakes in this book are baked in a half- or quarter-sheet pan and then cut into rounds with cutters of multiple sizes. To me, this is the only way to make a layer cake. Consider:

1. Fewer pans to wash.
2. Everything is perfectly even—you don't have to level the layers with a serrated knife.
3. You don't have to remove the cake from its pan to cool; just cut the layers right out of the pan once the cake has cooled.
4. You get scraps! Scraps to eat (you'll want to sample the goods, right?), scraps to experiment with, or even scraps to make an entire mini cake.
5. There will be no browned or burnt edges to trim (see opposite).
6. With a clean edge, you don't have to frost the sides of the cake if you don't want to.

Mini springform pans (3½-inch diameter)
Standard cupcake pan (24 count)
Mini cupcake pan (96 count)
Standard muffin tin (12 count)
Standard loaf pan (9 x 5 x 3 inches)
Mini loaf pan (5¾ x 3¼ x 2¼ inches)
Large Bundt pan (10 to 15 cups) ←
Medium Bundt pan (6 cups)
Mini Bundt pan (1 cup)
Doughnut pan (12 count)
Mini doughnut pan (108 count)

A Bundt pan is great when you want the cake to be the star.

CAKE ROUNDS, BROWN PARCHMENT PAPER, WAX PAPER. Lining a baking pan with buttered parchment or wax paper not only makes the pan easier to clean, but also prevents a crust on the cake edges. (I also really love peeling the parchment off the cake after it's baked. It's an "ahhh" moment for me.) Brown parchment also covers the counter and serves as the surface for making brittles (see page 255). Precut rounds of parchment paper, available in standard cake pan sizes, are just easy.

CUPCAKE LINERS. They make cleanup a cinch, but you don't have to use them (I often use butter in their place). It's your choice.

CUTE HEATPROOF TOWELS AND OVEN MITTS. Because, duh.

WIRE COOLING RACKS. Have at least one, but three are better if you are baking masses of cupcakes.

ROUND CAKE CUTTERS. I bake my layer cakes in a sheet pan and use these to cut out the layers. Cake cutters can be bought in sets or individually, online or at baking supply or craft stores. They range in size from ⅞ of an inch to 12 inches in diameter (and come in many shapes other than circles, too).

LAYER YOUR CAKES

When you are cutting a cake to make one thick layer into two, place the cake on a turntable and gently turn the table while letting the edge of a serrated knife gently make a ½-inch-deep cut around the entire cake. Once you have an even line, you can finish the cut horizontally through the layer, continuing to turn the table as you cut.

Level the layers of a cake in the same way, slicing off the center mound where the cake has risen. This, however, is why I think sheet pans are the way to go—you don't have to level the layers. Trying to level never comes out perfect and you have to deal with more crumbs when you're icing the cake.

PASTRY BRUSH. Useful for buttering the nooks and crannies of odd-shaped pans and for brushing crumbs from the cake surface.

PAIRING KNIFE, CHEF'S KNIFE, SERRATED KNIFE, X-ACTO KNIFE, LONG METAL RULER, AND SCISSORS. For trimming, chopping, cutting, measuring, and endless other little tasks, these basics are good to have in any kitchen.

STORAGE CANISTERS FOR FLOUR AND SUGAR. I'm not very neat in the kitchen, but these help keep things from getting messy. Scoop or spoon the ingredients into a dry measuring cup and level the top with the back of a knife. I also keep lidded plastic quart and pint containers on hand. They're handy for holding icing, toppings, and crumbles.

PLASTIC WRAP. It's a staple for all the obvious reasons, but especially for wrapping a cake before freezing.

CAKE TURNTABLE. A turntable isn't essential, but it definitely makes icing a cake easier, especially with ombre colors. If you have a lazy Susan in your pantry, you could set a cake plate on top of it and use it in a pinch.

CARDBOARD CAKE ROUNDS. Very helpful for moving a cake from the freezer to the turntable and from the turntable to the cake plate.

DISPOSABLE LATEX GLOVES. Trust me, they make many kitchen tasks much easier. Baking and cake decorating are very hands-on, and with gloves, you don't have to keep washing your hands. I also wear them to butter baking pans—there is no better tool than your hands. I don't like powder-free latex gloves, personally. The latex gloves with powder slide on and off so easily and I've found that they clean your jewelry while you wear them. My engagement ring is always sparkling after I take them off!

SMALL AND LARGE OFFSET SPATULAS.
These make spreading and icing easier, but you can always use a knife.

BENCH SCRAPER. I use a bench scraper to get a nice smooth coat of icing. It's also useful for crumb coating (see page 42) and ombre icing (see page 42). Choose a straight one, not one that's bent for scooping. If you don't have one, a straight metal ruler will work, too.

DISPOSABLE PLASTIC PIPING BAGS. I love disposable pastry bags. I think that part of what deters some people from baking is all the cleanup involved. Using pastry bags is messy enough already, so it's great if you can throw them away when you're done. These bags are inexpensive and give better control than plastic storage bags. Use them for piping icing, stuffing cupcakes (see page 272), or making The Tie-Dye Cake (page 37).

THE FREEZER IS A TOOL!

I consider the freezer section of my fridge to be an essential piece of equipment. You can bake cakes up to two weeks ahead of time, freeze them, and decorate them right before serving and no one will know. I also hold cake layers in the freezer while I'm in the process of icing. It's easier to frost a cold cake. You should use your freezer between steps to make sure you're working with cold cakes.

VARIOUS PIPING TIPS. You can simply cut off the tip of a plastic piping bag to pipe icing, but a set of tips is nice to have for special effects.

SKEWERS. I use thin bamboo skewers for making designs from different colored batters, especially in the Tie-Dye Cake (page 37).

SIFTER OR FINE-MESH SIEVE. For dusting a cake with confectioners' sugar or cocoa powder.

IN THE PANTRY

If you look in my pantry, you'll find things like peanut butter, Marshmallow Fluff, and brownie mix. It's no coincidence that these ingredients are in many of the recipes that follow. That's because these are foods that my family and I love. Take a look in your pantry and you'll find it's the same: it's filled with foods that you and your family enjoy eating over and over again.

The following items are staples that I always have on hand for baking, but I challenge you to be resourceful in your own kitchen. Take the ingredients you have and put them to use for a kick-butt dessert or cake that makes your family feel like they've been eating it all their lives.

FLOUR. I use all-purpose flour for baking.

SUGAR. Granulated sugar, confectioners' sugar, and dark and light brown sugars.

Keep a piece of white bread in the canister with your brown sugar and it won't harden.

BUTTER. Use a good-quality unsalted butter. I use a lot of butter. It keeps well in the freezer, so stock up when it's on sale.

EGGS. I use large eggs.

PURE VANILLA EXTRACT. It's in almost every cake, so keep a large bottle on hand.

MILK AND OTHER DAIRY. Always use whole milk and full-fat dairy (especially cream cheese). It's cake—why would you try to cut back on the calories?

FINE AND COARSE SEA SALT. Just like in savory cooking, salt brings all of the flavors together. I use fine sea salt in almost every cake recipe and coarse sea salt as a garnish.

COCOA POWDER. Always unsweetened. I don't get fancy here: use whatever brand you like.

MICRO CHOCOLATE CHIPS. I like to use micro chocolate chips, but they can be difficult to find (www.chocosphere.com is one online source). You can use mini or regular chocolate chips instead.

BAKER'S CHOCOLATE. For melting, brittles, and drizzles. Use whatever kind you like, but I prefer the wafers.

If you want a more liquid texture in your melted chocolate, add a little bit of vegetable oil.

FOOD COLORING. I use food coloring to make sure the cake looks the way I want it to. I love the Amerigel brand because its colors are brighter, but any brand will do the job.

SPRINKLES, NONPAREILS, AND SANDING SUGAR. Nothing makes me happier than walking the aisles of a baking supply store and filling my basket with as many different colors as I can find. I am never without sprinkles.

WHOLE MILK VERSUS BUTTERMILK

Milk adds creaminess to a cake, while buttermilk adds tang to the flavor and tenderness to the texture. I use whole milk, but give buttermilk a try and see how you like it. Bonus: you can freeze buttermilk (pour it into a cupcake pan, freeze it, and then store the rounds in a plastic bag), so it's always on hand if you run out of fresh milk.

Traditional buttermilk is the liquid left behind after cream has been separated from whole milk, but what you'll find in stores is low-fat milk with added cultures. If you'd like to make your own, add 1 tablespoon lemon juice to 1 cup whole milk and let the mixture sit until it curdles (about 10 minutes).

BROWNIE MIX AND STORE-BOUGHT COOKIE DOUGH. Keep these on hand for brownie batter and cake batter icings, as well as my Slutty Cake layers (see page 275). Use your favorite brand, but follow the package sizes given with each recipe.

PEANUT BUTTER, JELLIES AND JAMS, MARSH-MALLOW FLUFF, AND NUTELLA. These are pantry essentials at my house. Any one of these items can stuff or frost a cupcake or cake, so why would you want to be without them? I like the pure peanut butters, the ones whose labels list just peanuts and salt.

MELISSA'S TIPS
FOR EASY, DELICIOUS BAKING

• Always have all your ingredients at room temperature before you start baking.

• When measuring sticky ingredients like peanut butter, Marshmallow Fluff, or honey, spray the measuring cup with nonstick spray so the ingredients release easily.

• Level off dry ingredients with the back of a butter knife.

• When adding ingredients like confectioners' sugar or milk to the mixer bowl, always start on the lowest speed so you don't get splashed.

• Don't forget to add salt. It brings all the flavors together.

• Don't overmix—stop the mixer as soon as you have a smooth batter.

• Use disposable pastry bags to put batter in smaller baking pans. It works much better than a spoon.

• Each brand of food coloring is different, so always add the color last, one drop at a time. Be creative with color—make it your own.

• Line the cake pan with parchment and butter the pan and the parchment. I'm not a crust person and I find that lining the pan keeps the whole cake a little softer. You don't have to do this; it's easier to just spray the pan. But I also love the sensation of pulling the parchment away from the cake.

• For round cakes, use a sheet pan and cut the layers out with cake cutters in whatever size you want. Why clean three pans when you can clean only one? And who says a cake has to be 9 inches?

• Bundt pans are great for when you want the cake to be the hero. If you'd like, you can drizzle it with a little glaze.

- Tap the batter-filled pan on the counter—actually, drop it—a couple of times to pop any air bubbles that might be in the batter.

- If you're adding ingredients like chocolate chips or blueberries, let the cake bake for five to ten minutes, then sprinkle your add-ins over the top of the cake. That will keep them from sinking to the bottom.

- I never use a timer or a cake tester. A cake—in any form—is done when the cake springs back completely after you press your finger into the center. Don't poke it—just press it lightly onto the surface.

- The cake should be completely cooled before you apply any topping. Stick it in the freezer if you're impatient like me.

- If you're not serving the cake right away, wrap the unfrosted layers tightly in plastic wrap and store them in the freezer. They'll stay fresh for up to two weeks.

- Keep extra layers and any extra icing in the fridge or freezer while icing. A cold cake won't melt the icing.

- Don't stress over cracks or surface imperfections. Icing and glazes cover everything.

- When making glazes, do not add the entire milk measurement at once. Consistency and how much drip you want should be your guide. More milk makes the glaze thinner and the drip will travel all the way down to the bottom of the cake; less milk gives the glaze a much thicker consistency and it will fall just over the edges (see page 217).

- If your crumbles aren't holding together, add a little more melted butter for bigger chunks.

I don't follow recipes,

or at least I rarely do. Part of that comes from experience, but also . . . Google. We live in an age when you have no excuse not to be able to do anything. If there's something I want to make but I've never baked it before, I'll read a ton of recipes online so that I understand it. Chances are, I'll use a recipe the first time—but that's it. After that, everything's open to interpretation.

Once you get the concept down, you can create any kind of variation on that concept. That's how I create every single flavor at Baked by Melissa: if I love it, I'm going to figure out how to make it work as a cupcake, as a macaron, or as a muffin. The recipes that follow will give you the power to create what you love, too.

My Classic Vanilla Cake (page 34) is delicious. It's not too sweet and it's the perfect canvas for thousands of cakes. With Chocolate Glaze (page 222) and Coconut Goo (page 245), it's a Samoa cake that tastes just like your favorite Girl Scout cookie. Replace some of the liquid in the recipe with strawberry puree, and you have a delicious Strawberry Cake (page 55) that's bursting with fruit flavor. Stuff it with Cream Cheese Icing (page 185) and frost it with Chocolate Icing (page 168). Are Oreos more your thing? Make my Grandma Annie's Chocolate Cake (page 89), stuff it with Cookies and Cream Icing (page 176), frost it with Vanilla Icing (page 161), and you have the perfect balance of flavors that makes you think of cookies and cream ice cream.

While some people say, "Baking is chemistry; you have to make sure that everything is exact," I am here to tell you that's not true—trust me, it's not. You just have to have a slightly educated starting point. If you're adding a flavor that's a liquid, reduce the liquid in the base recipe. If you're adding a dry blend of something like coconut, hold back on the flour.

All of these recipes are super simple—and they're written in the same way I think about

CAKE WAFFLES

You can use any of the cake recipes to make twelve delicious waffles by adding 1 additional cup of all-purpose flour to the batter. (The added flour isn't absolutely necessary, but it will yield a thicker waffle.) Drop the batter onto the waffle iron ½ cup at a time and bake according to your waffle iron directions (about 2 minutes per waffle).

putting things together. I want you to think that way too: learn one recipe and the possibilities are endless.

Use this collection to go deeper into flavor profiles and you'll learn how you can relate them to other delicious foods you love. Do you love cinnamon? Make a Cinnamon Cake (page 60) with Cinnamon Icing (page 171). Or turn it into coffee cake with Cinnamon Crumble (page 243) baked into it and white chocolate drizzle (page 259) on top. Or frost that cake with Vanilla Icing (page 161) and you have the flavors of a cinnamon bun. Combining different flavor profiles will give your cakes greater depth of taste. Try Grandma Annie's Chocolate Cake (page 89) with Peanut Butter Icing (page 174).

Anything can be a cake—so begin by asking yourself, "What are my favorite flavors?" Then pick some of those for the cake, filling, and icing—the result will knock your socks off. If there's someone you love and care about and you want to do something special for them, make them something unique: a cake based on what *they* love. As you know, my original tie-dye cupcakes were a birthday gift to a friend who loved all things Grateful Dead.

Whether you're making a cake for your family or for friends (or even for yourself), it's a gift and it's the best way to show you care. When you put time and thought into a cake, it shows a commitment, and people don't do enough of that anymore. I get so much joy from baking for others, both at home and at Baked by Melissa. I want you to share in that experience.

Bake without fear. As president of the company and the face of the brand as well as the product, I'm forced to go outside my comfort zone every day. But I see challenges as opportunities, and that directly translates to my craft and why I'm good at baking. Many of the most amazing things I've ever created in the kitchen were the result of my attempts to cover up mistakes. Maybe I wouldn't have gone home and baked cupcakes if I hadn't been fired, and maybe I wouldn't have put a glaze on top of a cake if I hadn't burned it.

Think of these recipes as your canvas and paints— go create.

HOW MANY SERVINGS?

It's always difficult to say how many servings you'll get from one cake: some people want only a sliver, some want a big slice, and some want the whole cake. Each of the batter recipes in this book will make one 9 x 13-inch sheet cake, two 9-inch rounds, three 8-inch rounds—all of which can serve up to sixteen people—or two dozen standard cupcakes.

THE FINGERPRINT TEST

When checking to see if a cake is done, I always take it out of the oven with a pot holder and test it with my finger. As long as the cake bounces right back up and there's no fingerprint left behind, it's done. If your finger makes a little mark, put the cake back in the oven for a few minutes because it's not done. If you take it out too soon, it will sink.

CAKE BAKING TIMES AND RECIPE YIELDS

In terms of yields, I stand by the "everyone is different" out look. A serving for me would be 5 servings for my mom. A quarter sheet could serve about 15 people. A half sheet could serve 30 people. Small individual cakes could serve 1 person each—unless they're the mini versions, in which case I would suggest two minis per person. Unless I tell you otherwise, use this chart for the yields and approximate baking times for all of the cake recipes that follow. Remember, all ovens are different, so be sure to test your cake for doneness using the fingerprint test on the facing page.

PAN	CAKE	BAKING TIME
Half-sheet pan (13 x 18 inches)	1	30 to 35 minutes
Quarter-sheet pan (9 x 13 inches)	2	30 to 35 minutes
9-inch round cake pans	2	35 to 40 minutes
Mini springform pans (3½-inch diameter)	8	30 to 35 minutes
Standard cupcake pan (24 count)	24	25 to 30 minutes
Mini cupcake pan (96 count) *I recommend cutting the recipe in half and making only 48 cupcakes.*	96	15 to 18 minutes
Standard muffin tin (12 count)	12	25 to 30 minutes
Standard loaf pans (9 x 5 x 3 inches)	2	50 to 60 minutes
Mini loaf pans (5¾ x 3¼ x 2¼ inches)	16	25 to 30 minutes
Large Bundt pan (10 to 15 cup)	1	60 to 70 minutes
Medium Bundt pans (6 cups)	4	30 minutes
Mini Bundt pans (1 cup)	12	25 to 30 minutes
Doughnut pan (12 count)	12	20 to 25 minutes
Mini doughnut pan (108 count) *I recommend cutting the recipe in half and making only 54 doughnuts.*	108	15 minutes

BATTERS

CLASSIC VANILLA CAKE

This vanilla cake is the perfect canvas. It's not too sweet, but it's full of vanilla flavor. I have a vivid image of baking with my mother when I was a kid, watching her pour the vanilla extract into the spoon and letting it overflow into the bowl. That's what I do, too. You can add any sweet ingredients to this cake—like strawberry puree (page 53) or micro chocolate chips (page 24)—and they won't be overwhelming; in fact, with any added ingredient, whatever flavor you choose will shine through.

For best results, have all your ingredients at room temperature.

½ pound (2 sticks) unsalted butter, plus more for greasing the pan

2 cups sugar

2 teaspoons pure vanilla extract

4 large eggs

3 cups all-purpose flour

2 teaspoons baking powder

¼ teaspoon sea salt

1¾ cups whole milk (or buttermilk; let the cup overflow a bit)

Let it overflow the spoon if you want.

Salt brings all the flavors together.

Milk adds creaminess; buttermilk will add tang and tenderness.

1. Preheat the oven to 350°F. Butter the pan of your choice (see page 31) or line the pan with wax paper or parchment and butter the paper. This will make the edges *less* crispy. (I'm not an edge girl; I like the middle of the cake.)

2. With a hand mixer or a stand mixer fitted with the paddle attachment, whip the butter for 1 minute on high speed, then scrape down the sides of the bowl with a spatula. Add the sugar and beat on high speed for 2 minutes. Scrape down the sides of the bowl again.

3. Add the vanilla extract. While mixing at medium-low speed, add the eggs one at a time. Scrape down the edges of the bowl midway through.

4. Combine the flour, baking powder, and sea salt in a separate bowl.

5. With the mixer on low speed, add half the flour mixture. When it's mostly incorporated, add half the milk. Add the remainder of the dry and wet ingredients, scraping down the sides of the bowl between additions. Stop mixing as soon as you have a smooth batter.

6. Take the paddle attachment off the mixer and lick the batter—it should be delicious!

↳ Don't do this if you're pregnant or have a compromised immune system.

7. Pour the batter into the prepared pan and bake until the middle of the cake feels springy when you gently press your finger against it (see page 31 for approximate baking times). All ovens are different, so it's important to do the fingerprint test (see page 30) to see if the cake is done.

8. Let the cake cool completely before icing.

You're welcome!

THE TIE-DYE CAKE

CAKE: **Classic Vanilla Cake**

FILLING: **Vanilla Icing**

ICING: **Vanilla Icing**

GLAZE: **Vanilla Glaze**

TOPPING: **Rainbow sprinkles**

To me, tie-dye represents everything that's great in this world: diverse in color, fun, beautiful, delicious, and heartwarming. One of the original Baked by Melissa cupcakes, tie-dye is the arts-and-crafts project that you can eat.

I usually do five colors for the tie-dye cake—four is fine, five is fun, but I wouldn't do more than that. You could also do Funfetti as your fifth color. I've done that and it's really cute. The trick is not to futz around too much after you have the batter in the pan—the more colors you have and the more you mix them, the greater the chance of overmixing and turning everything brown.

2 recipes Classic Vanilla Cake (page 34)

1 recipe Vanilla Icing (page 161)

1 recipe Vanilla Glaze (page 218)

Pink, green, yellow, orange, and blue food coloring (or the colors of your choice)

1. Preheat the oven to 350°F. Butter three 9-inch round cake pans or line them with wax paper or parchment and butter the paper.

2. Divide the cake batter evenly among five small bowls. Add food coloring to each bowl—1 drop at a time—until the desired intensity of each color is reached. Scoop each color into a disposable pastry bag and snip the tip of the bag. I tie the ends of the pastry bags with plastic wrap or rubber bands to keep the batter in. Pipe the batter into the first pan, one color at a time, one over the next. (You could also use a spoon, but the pastry bags make this much easier.) Repeat with the remaining two pans. (This is the Zebra Cake technique. Search Pinterest for a full tutorial.)

3. To make the tie-dye effect, carefully drag a skewer completely through the batter from the center out to create a pattern with the colors. Don't overmix the colors.

4. Bake until the middle of the cake feels springy when you gently press your finger against it (see page 30), 35 to 40 minutes.

5. Set the cake aside to cool completely. Meanwhile, make the vanilla icing.

6. Level the cakes with a serrated knife (see page 21). Place one layer on a cake turntable and frost the top with the icing. Add the second cake layer and frost the top. Place the third layer on top and cover the entire cake with a "crumb coat" of white vanilla icing. I do a crumb coat—a thin layer of icing spread around the cake to seal in all the crumbs and ensure a neat finish. Unless it's a chocolate cake, the crumb coat is done with vanilla icing. It looks so clean and creates a nice blank canvas for decorating. If, instead, I have chocolate

(continues on page 42)

(continues from page 38)

icing on a chocolate cake, or I'm adding glazes or covering the whole cake with sprinkles, I might not care so much about the crumb coat, but it's really up to you.

7. Make the vanilla glaze to a thicker consistency than you want on the cake and divide it between two mixing bowls. Add pink food coloring to one bowl and blue food coloring to the other bowl—1 drop at a time—until the desired intensity of each color is reached. The food coloring will thin out the glaze a bit. You can always add more milk, but you can't take it away. Working with an offset spatula, spread pink glaze over the top of the cake and let it drip down the sides. Spread the blue glaze over the pink, but do not let it completely cover the pink. Finally, spoon more pink glaze onto the center of the cake top. Alternate the glazes just like you did with the batter. Use a skewer to pull the glaze from the center out to the edge and make the tie-dye design. Work quickly before the glaze starts to dry.

8. For tie-dye layer cakes, I always double the vanilla cake recipe. You lose some batter when mixing colors, and I like a slightly thicker cake so the beautiful colors really show. The doubled recipe will make two thick layers that can be stacked on top of one another or each sliced with a serrated knife to make four layers; you can also make one large 13 x 18-inch half-sheet pan and cut out cakes with round cutters.

9. I had no idea how I was going to decorate this cake when we brought it to the photo shoot. I made up the pink and blue glazes on the spot, and the result was so pretty. Always mix your glazes to a consistency that will give you the effect you want: Do you want the drips to go all the way down the sides of the cake? Halfway down? Or just stay on top? The amount of milk needed to achieve the desired consistency will vary, so add it slowly, one tablespoon at a time. The more milk added, the drippier the glaze. For the yellow ombre–frosted cake, I didn't want much drip—just a glistening coat that looked like shellac, so I didn't mix in as much milk. The pink and blue glazes have a little more milk.

10. To create the pink and yellow ombre icing, I fill one pastry bag with yellow-dyed vanilla icing and another with pink-dyed vanilla icing. With the cake on a turntable, I deposit a little ribbon of yellow and a little ribbon of pink as I turn the cake. I repeat the two ribbons, then take the bench scraper to smooth it all out.

VANILLA CUPCAKE WITH PB&J

CAKE: **Classic Vanilla Cake**   ICING: **Peanut butter**

FILLING: **Grape jelly**

I was so happy to make these cupcakes—and even happier to take a bite out of every one during the photo shoot. This is how we make our Baked by Melissa PB&J cupcakes—with real peanut butter for the icing. There's no other way to get an authentic flavor. The cupcakes are stuffed with store-bought grape jelly. That's what I grew up with, and I love it. You do what *you* love.

1 recipe Classic Vanilla Cake (page 34)	1½ cups store-bought grape jelly	One 16-ounce jar smooth peanut butter, preferably natural, at room temperature

1. Preheat the oven to 350°F. Butter a 24-count cupcake pan or line it with paper liners.

2. Mix the vanilla cake batter according to the recipe directions. Pour into the prepared pan and bake until the middle of a cupcake feels springy when you gently press your finger against it (see page 30), about 30 minutes.

3. Transfer the cupcakes to a rack to cool completely.

4. Fill a disposable pastry bag with the grape jelly. Massage the bag a bit before cutting off about ½ inch of the tip, so that you get an even mixture. With a small circular cookie cutter, cut a hole in the top of a cupcake and press open the edges. Slowly squeeze the bag to fill the cupcake with jelly. Repeat with the remaining cupcakes.

5. Fill another disposable pastry bag fitted with a round tip with peanut butter. Pipe a swirl on top of each cupcake, up and around but not covering the jam.

VANILLA CAKE WITH SUGAR COOKIE DOUGH

CAKE: **Classic Vanilla Cake**

ICING: **Vanilla Icing**

FILLING: **Sugar Cookie Dough Topping**

TOPPING: **Sanding sugar**

It's really easy to dress up a vanilla cake and turn it into something special. I'm not necessarily a vanilla person, but I do my happy dance when I eat this cake. Classic Vanilla Cake is stuffed and topped with Sugar Cookie Dough Topping. I add more heavy cream to the dough topping to make it easier to spread between the layers. The Vanilla Icing that frosts the cake keeps the surface very white so the colors of the sugar crystals really pop.

I love making my own sprinkle and sugar blends: it's just another way to have your personality shine through. To me, sugar cookie dough should be sprinkled with sanding sugar on the outside, and the colors shown on the cupcakes here are the colors that felt pretty on the day of the photo shoot. You can buy different colors of sanding sugar, sprinkles, and nonpareils at your local baking supply store or order them online.

1 recipe Classic Vanilla Cake (page 34)

1 recipe Sugar Cookie Dough Topping (page 244)

1 recipe Vanilla Icing (page 161)

Heavy cream, as needed

½ cup sanding sugar in the color mixture of your choice

1. Preheat the oven to 350°F. Butter a 13 x 18-inch half-sheet pan, then line it with wax paper or parchment and butter the paper.

2. Mix the cake batter according to the recipe directions. Pour into the prepared pan and bake until the middle of the cake feels springy when you gently press your finger against it (see page 30), about 40 minutes.

3. Let the cake cool completely in the pan. Using a 6-inch round cutter, cut 4 round layers from the sheet cake.

4. Meanwhile, make the cookie dough topping and the vanilla icing according to the recipe instructions. Divide the topping in half and place in separate bowls. Add more heavy cream, 1 tablespoon at a time, to one bowl until you reach a spreadable consistency.

5. Place one cake layer on a turntable and frost the top with about a third of the thinned cookie dough topping; repeat with the second and third layers. Place the top layer and frost the entire cake with the vanilla icing. Smooth the surface with a bench scraper.

6. Cover the cake with the sanding sugar, pressing the granules lightly into the sides. Using your clean hands, pinch small pieces of the unthinned sugar cookie dough topping and place them in a ring around the top of the cake.

BROWN SUGAR CAKE

I walk a little over a mile to the train station for my daily commute—a favorite time because I get a chance to clear my head. One morning I started thinking about brown sugar—I love it and I'll put it in anything anytime I can. The biggest difference between sugar cookies and chocolate chip cookies is the brown sugar—so rich and delicious. I wondered what would happen if I replaced the granulated sugar in my Classic Vanilla Cake with brown sugar. The result was a delicious cake. Brown sugar is simply granulated sugar with molasses in it, but that extra depth of flavor is really special.

Depending on your preference, you may decide the brown sugar cake is your favorite version of vanilla cake and use that as your base for other flavors. I use it as a base for flavor profiles that lend themselves to brown sugar, like the Pumpkin Spice and Pumpkin Spice Latte Cakes, because brown sugar has a certain warmth and feels like fall to me.

½ pound (2 sticks) unsalted butter, plus more for greasing the pan

2 cups packed light brown sugar

2 teaspoons pure vanilla extract

4 large eggs

3 cups all-purpose flour

2 teaspoons baking powder

¼ teaspoon fine sea salt

1¾ cups whole milk (or buttermilk)

1. Have all your ingredients at room temperature. Preheat the oven to 350°F. Butter the pan of your choice or line the pan with wax paper or parchment and butter the paper.

2. With a hand mixer or a stand mixer fitted with the paddle attachment, whip the butter for 1 minute on high speed, then scrape down the sides of the bowl with a spatula.

3. Add the sugar to the butter and beat on high speed for 2 minutes. Scrape down the sides of the bowl again.

4. With the mixer on medium-low speed, add the vanilla; then add the eggs one at a time. Scrape down the sides of the bowl midway through.

5. Combine the flour, baking powder, and sea salt in a separate bowl.

6. With the mixer on low speed, add half the flour mixture. When it's mostly incorporated, add half the milk. Add the remainder of the dry and wet ingredients, scraping

down the sides of the bowl between additions. Stop mixing as soon as you have a smooth batter.

7. Pour the batter into the prepared pan and bake until the middle of the cake feels springy when you gently press your finger against it (see page 31 for approximate baking times). All ovens are different, so it's important to do the fingerprint test (see page 30) to see if the cake is done.

8. Let the cake cool completely before icing.

STRAWBERRY CAKE

I don't put fruit in my salad, and I don't put fruit in my dessert—it doesn't belong there. But this strawberry cake? It's freakin' delicious. I wanted to develop a strawberry cupcake for Baked by Melissa and it took me a long time to figure it out. When I finally did, it was so simple—you replace the liquid in the Classic Vanilla Cake recipe with strawberry puree. You get a really bold flavor. I realized I could do that with any kind of fruit—and you can too. Ironically, this is one of my favorite recipes in this book.

½ pound (2 sticks) unsalted butter, plus more for greasing the pan

2 cups sugar

2 teaspoons pure vanilla extract

4 large eggs

3 cups all-purpose flour

2 teaspoons baking powder

¼ teaspoon fine sea salt

½ cup whole milk

1¾ cups strawberry puree (see Note)

1. Have all your ingredients at room temperature. Preheat the oven to 350°F. Butter the pan of your choice or line the pan with wax paper or parchment and butter the paper.

2. With a hand mixer or a stand mixer fitted with the paddle attachment, whip the butter for 1 minute on high speed, then scrape down the sides of the bowl with a spatula. Add the sugar and beat on high speed for 2 minutes. Scrape down the sides of the bowl again.

3. With the mixer on medium-low speed, add the vanilla extract; then add the eggs one at a time. Scrape down the sides of the bowl midway through.

4. Combine the flour, baking powder, and sea salt in a separate bowl. In another bowl, stir together the milk and the strawberry puree.

5. With the mixer on low speed, add half the flour mixture. When it's mostly incorporated, add half the milk mixture. Add the remainder of the dry and wet ingredients, scraping down the sides of the bowl between additions. Stop mixing as soon as you have a smooth batter.

6. Pour the batter into the prepared pan and bake until the middle of the cake feels springy when you gently press your finger against it (see page 31 for approximate baking times). All ovens are different, so it's important to do the fingerprint test (see page 30) to see if the cake is done.

7. Let the cake cool completely before icing.

NOTE

· ·

To make 1¾ cups strawberry puree, clean and hull 3½ cups (a little more than a pint) of fresh strawberries (they have more flavor than frozen). Puree the strawberries in a blender or food processor, adding a little granulated sugar if the berries are a bit tart.

STRAWBERRY CAKE

CAKE: **Strawberry Cake (page 55)**

FILLING: **Strawberry Cheesecake Icing (page 193)**

ICING: **Vanilla Icing (page 161)**

TOPPING: **Funfetti Crumble (page 243)**

My husband, Adi, and I gave Scottie a chance to enjoy a cupcake to distract her from the cake. The pink cake at the centerpiece is Strawberry Cake filled with Strawberry Cheesecake Icing. It's frosted with Vanilla Icing that's dyed with pink food coloring and topped with Funfetti Crumble.

LEMON CAKE

The freshness of lemon is really delicious—I put lemon in much of what I cook at home because it brightens things up. My lemon cake is fluffy and delicious, with the perfect amount of lemon flavor.

½ pound (2 sticks) unsalted butter, plus more for greasing the pan

2 cups sugar

¼ cup grated lemon zest

2 teaspoons pure vanilla extract

4 large eggs

3 cups all-purpose flour

2 teaspoons baking powder

¼ teaspoon fine sea salt

1¾ cups whole milk

¼ cup freshly squeezed lemon juice

1. Have all your ingredients at room temperature. Preheat the oven to 350°F. Butter the pan of your choice or line the pan with wax paper or parchment and butter the paper.

2. With a hand mixer or a stand mixer fitted with the paddle attachment, whip the butter for 1 minute on high speed, then scrape down the sides of the bowl with a spatula.

3. Add the sugar to the butter and beat on high speed for 2 minutes. Scrape down the sides of the bowl again.

4. With the mixer on medium-low speed, add the lemon zest and vanilla; then add the eggs one at a time. Scrape down the sides of the bowl midway through.

5. Combine the flour, baking powder, and sea salt in a separate bowl. In another bowl, mix the milk and the lemon juice.

6. With the mixer on low speed, add half the flour mixture. When it's mostly incorporated, add half the milk mixture. Add the remainder of the dry and wet ingredients, scraping down the sides of the bowl between additions. Stop mixing as soon as you have a smooth batter.

7. Pour the batter into the prepared pan and bake until the middle of the cake feels springy when you gently press your finger against it (see page 31 for approximate baking times). All ovens are different, so it's important to do the fingerprint test (see page 30) to see if the cake is done.

8. Let the cake cool completely before icing.

LIMONANA CAKE

•••

CAKE: **Lemon Cake (opposite)
or Mint Leaf Cake (page 155)**

ICING: **Real Mint Icing (page 198)
or Lemon Icing (page 173)**

TOPPING: **Sanding sugar**

•••

I've learned a lot about food from my husband, Adi. My love for food has evolved since we've met, and he's made me an even better cook and baker because we're so fiercely competitive in the kitchen (both at home and in the Baked by Melissa bakery).

Adi is from Israel, and a popular drink there is *limonana* (*limon* is lemon and *nana* is mint). It's a delicious combination and I also love saying it.

You can pair lemon cake with mint icing, as we did here, or pair mint cake with lemon icing. This flavor combination offers a more sophisticated taste. My lemon cake is super fluffy, with just the right amount of lemon. I used a drop of yellow food coloring in the cake batter and two drops of green and one drop of yellow in the icing because I love the way the bright yellow cake and the lime-green icing look together. The top is covered in matching sanding sugar, which makes it sparkle. I happened upon the sugar when I was exploring the aisles of New York Cake and Baking Supplies one day and thought it was the perfect color to complement this icing. This is a great cake for people who say they don't like cake—it's light and refreshing.

GRANDMA SYLVIA'S BLUEBERRY CAKE

When I was growing up, my grandparents had a little bungalow in the Catskills, where my mother had gone every summer as a child. We used to go there every weekend during the summer, too. I'd pick blueberries with my grandma, and then we'd come upstairs and make her blueberry cake, a delicious vanilla cake with all the blueberries on top. This is my adaptation of my grandmother's recipe. It brings me right back to my childhood, in the country with my grandma and our freshly picked blueberries.

½ pound (2 sticks) unsalted butter, plus more for greasing the pan

2 cups sugar

2 teaspoons pure vanilla extract

4 large eggs

3 cups all-purpose flour

2 teaspoons baking powder

¼ teaspoon fine sea salt

1¾ cups whole milk

2 cups fresh blueberries, washed and dried

1. Have all your ingredients at room temperature. Preheat the oven to 350°F. Butter the pan of your choice or line the pan with wax paper or parchment and butter the paper.

2. With a hand mixer or a stand mixer fitted with the paddle attachment, whip the butter for 1 minute on high speed, then scrape down the sides of the bowl with a spatula.

3. Add the sugar to the butter and beat on high speed for 2 minutes. Scrape down the sides of the bowl again.

4. With the mixer on medium-low speed, add the vanilla; then add the eggs one at a time. Scrape down the sides of the bowl midway through.

5. Combine the flour, baking powder, and sea salt in a separate bowl.

6. With the mixer on low speed, add half the flour mixture. When it's mostly incorporated, add half the milk. Add the remainder of the dry and wet ingredients, scraping down the sides of the bowl between additions. Stop mixing as soon as you have a smooth batter. With a spatula, fold 1 cup of the blueberries into the batter.

7. Pour the batter into the prepared pan and bake for 5 minutes, then sprinkle the top with the remaining blueberries (they tend to sink to the bottom, and I think this cake should have blueberries poking through the top). Continue to bake until the middle of the cake feels springy when you gently press your finger against it (see page 31 for approximate baking times). All ovens are different, so it's important to do the fingerprint test (see page 30) to see if the cake is done.

8. Let the cake cool completely before icing.

CINNAMON CAKE

I love cinnamon. It pairs so well with peanut butter and chocolate. I made a chocolate babka cupcake for the Baked by Melissa March Mini of the Month in 2015 and it used cinnamon and chocolate. To me, cinnamon and chocolate equals babka, a dessert I grew up with that makes me feel happy inside when I eat it.

I put cinnamon in my banana cake and in my peanut butter; cinnamon graham crackers bring me back to my childhood. When I think about a cake I'm always thinking about the combinations. You could have a cinnamon cake with cinnamon icing, but you could also buy that at the store. Go deeper into flavor profiles and see how you can relate them to people or to other delicious foods that you love. For example, cinnamon cake with a vanilla glaze is a cinnamon bun—yum.

½ pound (2 sticks) unsalted butter, plus more for greasing the pan

2 cups packed light brown sugar

2 teaspoons pure vanilla extract

4 large eggs

3 cups all-purpose flour

2 teaspoons baking powder

1 tablespoon ground cinnamon

¼ teaspoon fine sea salt

1¾ cups whole milk

1. Have all your ingredients at room temperature. Preheat the oven to 350°F. Butter the pan of your choice or line the pan with wax paper or parchment and butter the paper.

2. With a hand mixer or a stand mixer fitted with the paddle attachment, whip the butter for 1 minute on high speed, then scrape down the sides of the bowl with a spatula.

3. Add the sugar to the butter and beat on high speed for 2 minutes. Scrape down the sides of the bowl again.

4. With the mixer on medium-low speed, add the vanilla; then add the eggs one at a time. Scrape down the sides of the bowl midway through.

5. Combine the flour, baking powder, cinnamon, and sea salt in a separate bowl.

6. With the mixer on low speed, add half the flour mixture. When it's mostly incorporated, add half the milk. Add the remainder of the dry and wet ingredients, scraping down the sides of the bowl between additions. Stop mixing as soon as you have a smooth batter.

7. Pour the batter into the prepared pan and bake until the middle of the cake feels springy when you gently press your finger against it (see page 31 for approximate baking times). All ovens are different, so it's important to do the fingerprint test (see page 30) to see if the cake is done.

8. Let the cake cool completely before icing.

CHOCOLATE CHIP CAKE

When I was growing up, my mom would buy Entenmann's Chocolate Chip Crumb Loaf Cake. That wasn't necessarily the inspiration for this cake when I first made it, but when I tasted it, I was like, "Holy crap! This is that cake!" Now when you go to your local supermarket and see this cake on the Entenmann's display, you'll think to yourself, "Oh my god, I know how to make it!"

½ pound (2 sticks) unsalted butter, plus more for greasing the pan

2 cups sugar

2 teaspoons pure vanilla extract

4 large eggs

3 cups all-purpose flour

2 teaspoons baking powder

¼ teaspoon fine sea salt

1¾ cups whole milk

1 cup micro chocolate chips (see page 24)

Use the smallest chocolate chips you can find.

1. Have all your ingredients at room temperature. Preheat the oven to 350°F. Butter the pan of your choice or line the pan with wax paper or parchment and butter the paper.

2. With a hand mixer or a stand mixer fitted with the paddle attachment, whip the butter for 1 minute on high speed, then scrape down the sides of the bowl with a spatula.

3. Add the sugar to the butter and beat on high speed for 2 minutes. Scrape down the sides of the bowl again.

4. With the mixer on medium-low speed, add the vanilla; then add the eggs one at a time. Scrape down the sides of the bowl midway through.

5. Combine the flour, baking powder, and sea salt in a separate bowl.

6. With the mixer on low speed, add half the flour mixture. When it's mostly incorporated, add half the milk. Add the remainder of the dry and wet ingredients, scraping down the sides of the bowl between additions. Stop mixing as soon as you have a smooth batter.

7. Pour the batter into the prepared pan and bake for 5 minutes. Sprinkle the chocolate chips over the top of the cake and return it to the oven. Bake until the middle of the cake feels springy when you gently press your finger against it (see page 31 for approximate baking times). All ovens are different, so it's important to do the fingerprint test (see page 30) to see if the cake is done.

8. Let the cake cool completely before icing.

CHOCOLATE CHIP LOAF CAKE

CAKE: **Chocolate Chip Cake**   TOPPINGS: **Chocolate Crumble, confectioners' sugar**

This is my version of the Entenmann's classic. The cake has a little extra butter, which makes it denser and richer. It really holds together with all the chocolate chips inside. I put the chocolate crumbs on top before baking the cake and then dust it with confectioners' sugar once it's cool.

This is one of my favorite recipes in the book. When we had finished photographing this cake, I didn't just eat a piece of it; I ate the whole thing.

1 recipe Chocolate Chip Cake (page 62)   **1 recipe Chocolate Crumble (page 243)**   **Confectioners' sugar, for dusting**

1. Preheat the oven to 350°F. Butter a 9-inch (6-cup) loaf pan, then line it with wax paper or parchment and butter the paper.

2. Mix the chocolate chip cake batter according to the recipe directions and pour into the prepared pan.

3. Make the chocolate crumble according to the recipe directions and sprinkle them over the batter to thickly cover the cake.

4. Bake until the middle of the cake feels springy when you gently press your finger against it (see page 30), 50 to 60 minutes.

5. Turn the cake out onto a rack to cool completely. Once it's cool, replace any crumble that may have fallen off, then dust the top of the cake with confectioners' sugar.

DOUGHNUT CAKE

I love doughnuts. But cake is already an indulgence, so why fry it too? There's a specific flavor that shines through when you eat a doughnut. Since I really wanted to enjoy a doughnut as cake, I figured out what that spice is—it's called mace. A little bit goes a long way, and if you add it to the Classic Vanilla Cake recipe, you're going to get a doughnut cake. And if you add mace to Vanilla Icing, you're going to get doughnut icing. I love watching people try this cake for the first time—they laugh and say, "That's a doughnut!" I can't wait for you to try it.

½ pound (2 sticks) unsalted butter, plus more for greasing the pan

2 cups sugar

2 teaspoons pure vanilla extract

4 large eggs

3 cups all-purpose flour

2 teaspoons baking powder

1¼ teaspoons ground mace (see Note)

¼ teaspoon fine sea salt

1¾ cups whole milk

1. Have all your ingredients at room temperature. Preheat the oven to 350°F. Butter the pan of your choice or line the pan with wax paper or parchment and butter the paper.

2. With a hand mixer or a stand mixer fitted with the paddle attachment, whip the butter for 1 minute on high speed, then scrape down the sides of the bowl with a spatula.

3. Add the sugar to the butter and beat on high speed for 2 minutes. Scrape down the sides of the bowl again.

4. With the mixer on medium-low speed, add the vanilla; then add the eggs one at a time. Scrape down the sides of the bowl midway through.

5. Combine the flour, baking powder, mace, and sea salt in a separate bowl.

6. With the mixer on low speed, add half the flour mixture. When it's mostly incorporated, add half the milk. Add the remainder of the dry and wet ingredients, scraping down the sides of the bowl between additions. Stop mixing as soon as you have a smooth batter.

7. Pour the batter into the prepared pan and bake until the middle of the cake feels springy when you gently press your finger against it (see page 31 for approximate baking times). All ovens are different, so it's important to do the fingerprint test (see page 30) to see if the cake is done.

8. Let the cake cool completely before icing.

NOTE

· ·

Mace is made from the covering of the nutmeg seed and has a similar aroma. You can use mace as a substitute for nutmeg, but don't use nutmeg as a substitute for mace in this recipe.

HOT COCOA CAKE

I love the chocolate at the bottom of a mug of hot cocoa. When I was a kid, I used to put three packets of cocoa mix in the mug and then add the hot water, but not stir it. I would just eat it with a spoon. If that's your favorite part of hot cocoa too, then this recipe is for you. I recommend pairing this cake with the Hot Cocoa Icing for the true experience. Because the Classic Vanilla Cake batter on which this cake is based is not very sweet, you can add ingredients like store-bought cocoa mix or fruit and they don't become overpowering.

½ pound (2 sticks) unsalted butter, plus more for greasing the pan

2 cups sugar

2 teaspoons pure vanilla extract

4 large eggs

3 cups all-purpose flour

½ cup store-bought hot cocoa mix

1 tablespoon unsweetened cocoa powder

2 teaspoons baking powder

¼ teaspoon fine sea salt

1¾ cups whole milk

1. Have all your ingredients at room temperature. Preheat the oven to 350°F. Butter the pan of your choice or line the pan with wax paper or parchment and butter the paper.

2. With a hand mixer or a stand mixer fitted with the paddle attachment, whip the butter for 1 minute on high speed, then scrape down the sides of the bowl with a spatula.

3. Add the sugar to the butter and beat on high speed for 2 minutes. Scrape down the sides of the bowl again.

4. With the mixer on medium-low speed, add the vanilla; then add the eggs one at a time. Scrape down the sides of the bowl midway through.

5. Combine the flour, hot cocoa mix, cocoa powder, baking powder, and sea salt in a separate bowl.

6. With the mixer on low speed, add half the flour mixture. When it's mostly incorporated, add half the milk. Add the remainder of the dry and wet ingredients, scraping down the sides of the bowl between additions. Stop mixing as soon as you have a smooth batter.

7. Pour the batter into the prepared pan and bake until the middle of the cake feels springy when you gently press your finger against it (see page 31 for approximate baking times). All ovens are different, so it's important to do the fingerprint test (see page 30) to see if the cake is done.

8. Let the cake cool completely before icing.

HOT COCOA CAKE

. . . .

CAKE: **Hot Cocoa Cake**

FILLING: **Hot Cocoa Icing**

ICING: **Hot Cocoa Icing**

TOPPINGS: **Marshmallow Fluff Glaze, Hot Cocoa Glaze, and marshmallows**

. . . .

This cake demonstrates how to have fun with all these combinations. The cake was a mess, but it was gorgeous—truly a work of art and so much fun to make! I didn't have a plan for how to decorate the cake, so when the camera and the lights were set up I made it up on the spot.

I cannot control myself around this cake. It tastes like the bottom of a mug of hot chocolate. That's because it's all hot cocoa—Hot Cocoa Cake, Hot Cocoa Icing between the layers and on top, plus Marshmallow Fluff Glaze and Hot Cocoa Glaze topped with real marshmallows—so delicious.

2 recipes Hot Cocoa Cake (page 68)

1 recipe Hot Cocoa Icing (page 186)

1 recipe Marshmallow Fluff Glaze (page 232)

1 recipe Hot Cocoa Glaze (page 231)

Full-size and mini marshmallows

1. Preheat the oven to 350°F. Butter two 13 x 18-inch half-sheet pans, or line them with wax paper or parchment and butter the paper.

2. Mix the cake batter according to the recipe directions. Pour into the prepared pans and bake until the middle of the cake feels springy when you gently press your finger against it (see page 30), about 40 minutes.

3. Let the cakes cool in the pans. Using an 8-inch round cutter, cut two round layers from each sheet cake.

4. Meanwhile, make the cocoa icing according to the recipe instructions.

5. Place one cake layer on a turntable and frost the top with icing; repeat with the second and third layers. Place the top layer and frost the entire cake with the remaining icing. Smooth the surface with a bench scraper.

6. Mix the Marshmallow Fluff and cocoa glazes according to the recipe instructions. Keep them both on the thicker side. Once the glaze drips from your spoon in a single ribbon, it's ready (see page 217).

7. Spoon some of the Marshmallow Fluff glaze on top of the cake and spread it until it begins to drip over the edge of the cake (nudge it with an offset spatula if necessary). Spoon some of the hot cocoa glaze over the marshmallow glaze and let it drip over the edge of the cake.

8. Repeat once more with the marshmallow and cocoa glazes, and then add a final layer of the marshmallow glaze.

9. Scatter large and mini marshmallows over the top and drizzle with the remaining hot cocoa glaze.

FUNFETTI CAKE

Funfetti Cake is simply Classic Vanilla Cake with sprinkles added to the batter. Everybody loves Funfetti and I wouldn't be true to myself or Baked by Melissa if I didn't include a recipe. This is for your friend who really likes vanilla but wants lots of color. Like the Tie-Dye Cake, it's fun—and great for baking with your kids.

½ pound (2 sticks) unsalted butter, plus more for greasing the pan

2 cups sugar

2 teaspoons pure vanilla extract

4 large eggs

3 cups all-purpose flour

2 teaspoons baking powder

¼ teaspoon fine sea salt

1¾ cups whole milk

1 cup rainbow sprinkles

1. Have all your ingredients at room temperature. Preheat the oven to 350°F. Butter the pan of your choice or line the pan with wax paper or parchment and butter the paper.

2. With a hand mixer or a stand mixer fitted with the paddle attachment, whip the butter for 1 minute on high speed, then scrape down the sides of the bowl with a spatula.

3. Add the sugar to the butter and beat on high speed for 2 minutes. Scrape down the sides of the bowl again.

4. With the mixer on medium-low speed, add the vanilla; then add the eggs one at a time. Scrape down the sides of the bowl midway through.

5. Combine the flour, baking powder, and sea salt in a separate bowl.

6. With the mixer on low speed, add half the flour mixture. When it's mostly incorporated, add half the milk. Add the remainder of the dry and wet ingredients, scraping down the sides of the bowl between additions. Stop mixing as soon as you have a smooth batter. With a spatula, fold in the rainbow sprinkles.

7. Pour the batter into the prepared pan and bake until the middle of the cake feels springy when you gently press your finger against it (see page 31 for approximate baking times). All ovens are different, so it's important to do the fingerprint test (see page 30) to see if the cake is done.

8. Let the cake cool completely before icing.

CEREAL CAKE

I love cereal—who doesn't? For a cereal cake, I use fun, brightly colored cereals, like Fruity Pebbles. You can use any kind you want, but it should be sugared. I encourage you to use your favorites with this cake, too.

Pulse the cereal in a food processor until it's the texture of sand with small pebbles in it (you can also place the cereal in a plastic bag and crush it with a rolling pin).

½ pound (2 sticks) unsalted butter, plus more for greasing the pan

2 cups sugar

2 teaspoons pure vanilla extract

4 large eggs

2½ cups all-purpose flour

1 cup ground Fruity Pebbles cereal

2 teaspoons baking powder

¼ teaspoon fine sea salt

1¾ cups whole milk

1. Have all your ingredients at room temperature. Preheat the oven to 350°F. Butter the pan of your choice or line the pan with wax paper or parchment and butter the paper.

2. With a hand mixer or a stand mixer fitted with the paddle attachment, whip the butter for 1 minute on high speed, then scrape down the sides of the bowl with a spatula.

3. Add the sugar to the butter and beat on high speed for 2 minutes. Scrape down the sides of the bowl again.

4. With the mixer on medium-low speed, add the vanilla; then add the eggs one at a time. Scrape down the sides of the bowl midway through.

5. Combine the flour, ground cereal, baking powder, and sea salt in a separate bowl.

6. With the mixer on low speed, add half the flour mixture. When it's mostly incorporated, add half the milk. Add the remainder of the dry and wet ingredients, scraping down the sides of the bowl between additions. Stop mixing as soon as you have a smooth batter.

7. Pour the batter into the prepared pan and bake until the middle of the cake feels springy when you gently press your finger against it (see page 31 for approximate baking times). All ovens are different, so it's important to do the fingerprint test (see page 30) to see if the cake is done.

8. Let the cake cool completely before icing.

THE CEREAL CAKE

CAKE: **Cereal Cake**

FILLINGS: **Vanilla Icing with pink food coloring, Cereal Crumble**

ICING: **Cereal Icing**

TOPPINGS: **Cereal Crumble, Fruity Pebbles, and Vanilla Glaze**

Fruity Pebbles appear in almost every aspect of this cake: the cake, the icing, and the toppings—with Vanilla Glaze as a stand-in for the milk and pink buttercream between the layers.

1 recipe Cereal Cake (page 79)

1 recipe Vanilla Icing (page 161)

1 recipe Cereal Icing (page 196)

1 recipe Cereal Crumble (page 243)

Pink food coloring

2 cups Fruity Pebbles cereal

1 recipe Vanilla Glaze (page 218)

1. Preheat the oven to 350°F. Butter a 13 x 18-inch half-sheet pan, then line it with wax paper or parchment and butter the paper.

2. Mix the cereal cake batter according to the recipe directions. Pour into the prepared pan and bake until the middle of the cake feels springy when you gently press your finger against it (see page 30), about 40 minutes. Set aside to cool

3. Meanwhile, make the vanilla and cereal icings and the cereal crumble. Add the food coloring to the vanilla icing drop by drop until you reach the desired shade of pink.

4. Use a 6-inch round cutter to cut three rounds from the cake. Place one cake layer on a turntable, frost with about half the pink icing, and sprinkle about a quarter of the cereal crumbs over the top; repeat with the second layer. Place the top layer and frost the entire cake with the cereal icing.

5. Decorate the top and sides of the cake with the remaining cereal crumbs and the Fruity Pebbles. Make the vanilla glaze and drizzle it over each piece of cake as you serve it. It's better to decorate all at once, but if you're assembling the cake the night before, I would hold off adding the cereal to the top until the day of.

DULCE DE LECHE CAKE

I love to work with dulce de leche, and if you want to make your own, follow the instructions in the Note. But my goal is to make your baking experience fun and light, so here's my advice: go to the supermarket and buy a can of dulce de leche. Any brand will do. I choose dulce de leche over caramel because it has a much deeper flavor, you don't have to use as much, and the color is beautiful and rich. The Salted Caramel Icing (page 183) is the way to go with this cake. Pairing it with chocolate and espresso is also delicious.

½ pound (2 sticks) unsalted butter, plus more for greasing the pan

2 cups packed light brown sugar

2 teaspoons pure vanilla extract

4 large eggs

3 cups all-purpose flour

2 teaspoons baking powder

1 teaspoon fine sea salt

1¾ cups whole milk

1 cup store-bought dulce de leche (see Note)

1. Have all your ingredients at room temperature. Preheat the oven to 350°F. Butter the pan of your choice or line the pan with wax paper or parchment and butter the paper.

2. With a hand mixer or a stand mixer fitted with the paddle attachment, whip the butter for 1 minute on high speed, then scrape down the sides of the bowl with a spatula.

3. Add the sugar to the butter and beat on high speed for 2 minutes. Scrape down the sides of the bowl again.

4. With the mixer on medium-low speed, add the vanilla; then add the eggs one at a time. Scrape down the sides of the bowl midway through.

5. Combine the flour, baking powder, and sea salt in a separate bowl.

6. With the mixer on low speed, add half the flour mixture. When it's mostly incorporated, add half the milk. Add the remainder of the dry and wet ingredients, scraping down the sides of the bowl between additions. Stop mixing as soon as you have a smooth batter. Add the dulce de leche and mix until incorporated.

7. Pour the batter into the prepared pan and bake until the middle of the cake feels springy when you gently press your finger against it (see page 31 for approximate baking times). All ovens are different, so it's important to do the fingerprint test (see page 30) to see if the cake is done.

8. Let the cake cool completely before icing.

NOTE

••

I can't imagine anything easier than buying a can of dulce de leche at the grocery store, but if you can't find it or really want to make your own, here's what to do: Remove the label from a can of sweetened condensed milk and place the unopened can on its side in a large pot. Fill the pot with water to cover the can by 2 inches and bring to a simmer. Let it simmer uncovered for 2 to 3 hours (the longer it cooks, the darker the dulce de leche will be), making sure that the can is always covered by water. Use tongs to remove the can from the water and set it on a rack to cool completely (don't open the can before it has cooled). Once it's cool, open the can and you have your very own homemade dulce de leche. You'll have more than you need for this recipe, so store what's left over in the fridge for up to 3 weeks, covered.

MATCHA CAKE

Do you know how matcha I love cake? I love it so much that I've made it five different ways!

I first got turned on to matcha, which is a variety of Japanese green tea, a few years ago when I introduced a matcha cupcake at Baked by Melissa for our Mother's Day collection. Now I drink it every day. It's healthy, it has caffeine, and it's delicious.

Different types of matcha will give you different shades of green. Ceremonial matcha is made from the younger matcha leaves and will produce a brighter green (it's also more expensive, so brace yourself). You can put a dot of green food coloring in the batter if you want, but I didn't do that here.

Matcha gives the cake a unique and delicious flavor—and it tastes like tea. It's a different flavor profile for me, a bit sophisticated. If you like desserts such as mochi or green tea ice cream, you're going to love this cake.

½ pound (2 sticks) unsalted butter, plus more for greasing the pan

2 cups sugar

2 teaspoons pure vanilla extract

4 large eggs

3 cups all purpose flour

½ cup matcha green tea powder

2 teaspoons baking powder

¼ teaspoon fine sea salt

¾ cups whole milk

1. Have all your ingredients at room temperature. Preheat the oven to 350°F. Butter the pan of your choice or line the pan with wax paper or parchment and butter the paper.

2. With a hand mixer or a stand mixer fitted with the paddle attachment, whip the butter for 1 minute on high speed, then scrape down the sides of the bowl with a spatula.

3. Add the sugar to the butter and beat on high speed for 2 minutes. Scrape down the sides of the bowl again.

4. With the mixer on medium-low speed, add the vanilla; then add the eggs one at a time. Scrape down the sides of the bowl midway through.

5. Combine the flour, matcha, baking powder, and sea salt in a separate bowl.

6. With the mixer on low speed, add half the flour mixture. When it's mostly incorporated, add half the milk. Add the remainder of the dry and wet ingredients, scraping down the sides of the bowl between additions. Stop mixing as soon as you have a smooth batter.

7. Pour the batter into the prepared pan and bake until the middle of the cake feels springy when you gently press your finger against it (see page 31 for approximate baking times). All ovens are different, so it's important to do the fingerprint test (see page 30) to see when the cake is done.

8. Let the cake cool completely before icing.

MATCHA CAKES

. . . .

CAKE: **Matcha Cake (opposite)**

FILLING: **Matcha Icing (page 188)**

ICINGS: **Matcha Icing (page 188) and Vanilla Icing (page 161)**

TOPPINGS: **Matcha Glaze (page 235) and Vanilla Glaze (page 218), matcha powder**

. . . .

Check out the variety in the photo on the next page. You can pair Matcha Cake with Matcha Icing (as I did with the layer cake at upper left), or use Matcha Glaze and pair it with Vanilla Glaze (as I did on the Bundt cakes and the doughnut cakes). The pink icing on the cupcakes is Vanilla Icing with just a touch of pink food coloring because I think the two colors look so nice together. I put plain matcha in a sifter to decorate the top of the layer cake. Baking is a way to exercise your creative outlet—this displays only a little of what you can do with just one recipe.

COFFEE CAKE

Brown sugar cake with espresso added—it's phenomenal! The batter tastes like melted coffee ice cream. It's soooo good. Some chocolate icing is all you need. My mom loves the Ben & Jerry's flavor Coffee Coffee Buzz Buzz. So when I first developed this recipe, I made it into a cupcake, stuffed it with salted dulce de leche, and topped it with chocolate icing for her. She loved it. That's what's so fun—you decide what you want to do.

½ pound (2 sticks) unsalted butter, plus more for greasing the pan

2 cups sugar

2 teaspoons pure vanilla extract

4 large eggs

3 cups all-purpose flour

2 teaspoons baking powder

¼ teaspoon fine sea salt

⅓ cup whole milk

1½ cups brewed espresso

1. Have all your ingredients at room temperature. Preheat the oven to 350°F. Butter the pan of your choice or line the pan with wax paper or parchment and butter the paper.

2. With a hand mixer or a stand mixer fitted with the paddle attachment, whip the butter for 1 minute on high speed, then scrape down the sides of the bowl with a spatula.

3. Add the sugar to the butter and beat on high speed for 2 minutes. Scrape down the sides of the bowl again.

4. With the mixer on medium-low speed, add the vanilla; then add the eggs one at a time. Scrape down the sides of the bowl midway through.

5. Combine the flour, baking powder, and sea salt in a separate bowl. In another bowl, mix the milk and espresso.

6. With the mixer on low speed, add half the flour mixture. When it's mostly incorporated, add half the milk mixture. Add the remainder of the dry and wet ingredients, scraping down the sides of the bowl between additions. Stop mixing as soon as you have a smooth batter.

7. Pour the batter into the prepared pan and bake until the middle of the cake feels springy when you gently press your finger against it (see page 31 for approximate baking times). All ovens are different, so it's important to do the fingerprint test (see page 30) to see if the cake is done.

8. Let the cake cool completely before icing.

GRANDMA ANNIE'S CHOCOLATE CAKE

This chocolate cake—my grandmother's recipe—is completely different from the others. My father's mother was an unbelievable baker. The smell of this batter brings me right back to my childhood. I could have just added cocoa to my vanilla cake, but this is the best chocolate cake I've ever had, and everyone needs to know how to make it. It's fluffy, it's delicious, and like the Classic Vanilla Cake, it's the perfect canvas.

½ pound (2 sticks) unsalted butter, plus more for greasing the pan

2 cups sugar

2 teaspoons pure vanilla extract

2 large eggs

3 cups all-purpose flour

⅔ cup unsweetened cocoa powder

2 teaspoons baking soda

¼ teaspoon fine sea salt

2 cups (16 ounces) sour cream

1. Have all your ingredients at room temperature. Preheat the oven to 350°F. Butter the pan of your choice or line the pan with wax paper or parchment and butter the paper.

2. With a hand mixer or a stand mixer fitted with the paddle attachment, whip the butter for 1 minute on high speed, then scrape down the sides of the bowl with a spatula. Add the sugar to the butter and beat on high speed for 2 minutes. Scrape down the sides of the bowl again.

3. With the mixer on medium-low speed, add the vanilla extract; then add the eggs one at a time. Scrape down the edges of the bowl midway through.

4. Combine the flour, cocoa powder, baking soda, and sea salt in a separate bowl.

5. With the mixer on low speed, add half the flour mixture. When it's mostly incorporated, add half the sour cream. Add the remainder of the dry and wet ingredients, scraping down the sides of the bowl between additions. Stop mixing as soon as you have a smooth batter.

6. Pour the batter into the prepared pan and bake until the middle of the cake feels springy when you gently press your finger against it (see page 31 for approximate baking times). All ovens are different, so it's important to do the fingerprint test (see page 30) to see if the cake is done.

7. Let the cake cool completely before icing.

PEANUT BUTTER CUP CUPCAKES AND CHOCOLATE PEANUT BUTTER CAKE

CAKE: **Grandma Annie's Chocolate Cake (page 89)**

FILLING: **Peanut butter**

ICING: **Chocolate Icing (page 168)**

GLAZE: **Peanut Butter Glaze I (page 237)**

TOPPING: **Coarse sea salt**

When you're using chocolate or peanut butter, a sprinkle of salt makes all the difference. I use coarse sea salt, but you can use whatever type you like. Peanut butter and chocolate is one of my favorite combinations. For the cupcakes, I stuffed chocolate cake with peanut butter, then piped chocolate icing around the peanut butter and sprinkled it with sea salt.

The cake is a double recipe of Grandma Annie's Chocolate Cake, baked in two 13 x 18-inch half-sheet pans and cut into four layers with an 8-inch round cutter. (More layers, more filling!) I spread peanut butter between the layers and frosted the cake with a thin layer of chocolate icing. Then I melted peanut butter in the microwave for a few seconds and drizzled it on top for the glaze. I finished with a sprinkle of coarse sea salt. A slice of this cake is all I need in life.

NEAPOLITAN CAKE

. . . .

CAKES: **Grandma Annie's Chocolate Cake, Strawberry Cake, and Classic Vanilla Cake**

FILLING: **Strawberry Icing**

ICINGS: **Strawberry, Vanilla, and Chocolate Icing**

TOPPING: **Pink sprinkles**

. . . .

This layer cake is a fun take on that trio of flavors: strawberry, vanilla, and chocolate. It has Strawberry Icing between the layers and ombréd icing on the outside.

½ recipe Grandma Annie's Chocolate Cake (page 89)

½ recipe Strawberry Cake (page 55)

½ recipe Classic Vanilla Cake (page 34)

1 recipe Strawberry Icing (page 172)

½ recipe Vanilla Icing (page 161)

½ recipe Chocolate Icing (page 168)

½ cup pink sprinkles

1. Preheat the oven to 350°F. Butter three 9-inch round cake pans or line them with wax paper or parchment and butter the paper.

2. Mix the chocolate, strawberry, and vanilla cake batters according to the recipe directions and pour into the three prepared pans. Bake until the middle of each cake feels springy when you gently press your finger against it (see page 30), about 40 minutes. Invert the cakes on a rack to cool completely.

3. Meanwhile, make the strawberry, vanilla, and chocolate icings. Place the chocolate cake layer on a turntable and frost the top with about a third of the strawberry icing. Repeat with the second, strawberry layer.

4. Place the third, vanilla layer on top and cover the cake with a coat of vanilla icing, spreading it more thickly on the top than the sides. Place the remaining strawberry icing and the chocolate icing in disposable pastry bags and snip the tips. Pipe a row of strawberry icing on the outside, around the middle of the cake, and a row of chocolate around the bottom. Spread the piped icing smooth with a bench scraper. Decorate the top edge of the cake with the sprinkles.

S'MORES CUPCAKES

• •

CAKE: **Grandma Annie's Chocolate Cake**

FILLING: **Marshmallow Fluff**

ICING: **Chocolate Icing**

TOPPINGS: **Marshmallows and graham cracker pieces**

• •

A Baked by Melissa original flavor, the S'mores Cupcake isn't always available, but I use every opportunity I can to bring it back. Each chocolate cupcake is stuffed with Marshmallow Fluff, topped with Chocolate Icing, and garnished with real marshmallows and graham cracker pieces. Be generous with the garnishes, as this is where you get the s'mores flavor. If you don't have a kitchen torch to stand in for the campfire flame, here's your excuse to get one.

1 recipe Grandma Annie's Chocolate Cake (page 89)	**One 7.5-ounce jar Marshmallow Fluff**	**1 sleeve graham crackers, broken into 1-inch pieces**
1 recipe Chocolate Icing (page 168)	**1 jumbo marshmallow or 3 or 4 mini marshmallows**	

1. Preheat the oven to 350°F. Butter a 12-count cupcake pan or line with paper liners.

2. Mix the chocolate cake batter according to the recipe directions. Pour into the prepared pan and bake until the middle of a cupcake feels springy when you gently press your finger against it (see page 30), about 30 minutes.

3. Invert the cupcakes on a rack to cool completely.

4. Meanwhile, make the chocolate icing according to the recipe directions.

5. Fill a disposable pastry bag with the Marshmallow Fluff. Cut a hole in the top of a cupcake with a small round cutter, pull the center piece out with your fingers, and press open the edges. Slowly squeeze the bag to fill the cupcake (see page 162). Repeat with the remaining cupcakes.

6. Fill another disposable pastry bag fitted with a round tip (I used an Ateco no. 808) with the chocolate icing. Pipe a swirl on top of each cupcake, covering the Fluff.

7. Top each cupcake with a marshmallow and a square of graham cracker. If you want, use a kitchen torch to carefully caramelize the garnishes until they are lightly toasted. It's not necessary, but it's totally fun.

GRANDMA ANNIE'S CHOCOLATE ESPRESSO CAKE

This is another of my grandmother's recipes—a chocolate cake with espresso added.

½ pound (2 sticks) unsalted butter, plus more for greasing the pan

2 cups sugar

2 teaspoons pure vanilla extract

2 large eggs

3 cups all-purpose flour

⅔ cup unsweetened cocoa powder

2 teaspoons baking soda

¼ teaspoon fine sea salt

2 cups (16 ounces) sour cream

½ cup brewed espresso, cooled

Don't have an espresso machine? Pick up an espresso from your local coffee shop.

1. Have all your ingredients at room temperature. Preheat the oven to 350°F. Butter the pan of your choice or line the pan with wax paper or parchment and butter the paper.

2. With a hand mixer or a stand mixer fitted with the paddle attachment, whip the butter for 1 minute on high speed, then scrape down the sides of the bowl with a spatula. Add the sugar and beat on high speed for 2 minutes. Scrape down the sides of the bowl again.

3. With the mixer on medium-low speed, add the vanilla extract; then add the eggs one at a time. Scrape down the sides of the bowl midway through.

4. Combine the flour, cocoa powder, baking soda, and sea salt in a separate bowl. In another bowl, stir together the sour cream and espresso.

5. With the mixer on low speed, add half the flour mixture. When it's mostly incorporated, add half the sour cream mixture. Add the remainder of the dry and wet ingredients, scraping down the sides of the bowl between additions. Stop mixing as soon as you have a smooth batter.

6. Pour the batter into the prepared pan and bake until the middle of the cake feels springy when you gently press your finger against it (see page 31 for approximate baking times). All ovens are different, so it's important to do the fingerprint test (see page 30) to see if the cake is done. Let the cake cool completely before icing.

CHOCOLATE ESPRESSO CRUMBLE CAKE

....

CAKE: **Grandma Annie's Chocolate Espresso Cake**

FILLING: **Whipped Salted Caramel Icing**

ICING: **Chocolate Espresso Icing**

TOPPINGS: **Chocolate Crumble and rainbow sprinkles and nonpareils**

....

This is a cake I love to share with my parents. It's inspired by my grandmother's chocolate cake. My father loves to make chocolate babka, and the chocolate crumble on this cake reminds me of the crumble he uses to top the babka dough before he bakes it. My crumbs don't need to be baked. I actually prefer them unbaked, but they work both ways. Of course I top the cake with sprinkles and nonpareils—that's the one thing on which my dad and I don't see eye to eye.

2 recipes Grandma Annie's Chocolate Espresso Cake (page 98)

1 recipe Whipped Salted Caramel Icing (page 207)

1 recipe Chocolate Espresso Icing (page 177)

1 recipe Chocolate Crumble (page 243)

½ cup rainbow sprinkles and nonpareils, mixed

1. Preheat the oven to 350°F. Butter three 9-inch round cake pans or line them with wax paper or parchment and butter the paper.

2. Mix the chocolate espresso cake batter according to the recipe directions and pour the batter into the prepared pans. Bake until the middle of the cake feels springy when you gently press your finger against it (see page 30), about 40 minutes.

3. Set the cakes aside to cool completely. The cakes will cool faster out of the pan. I usually store cakes in the freezer until I assemble them.

4. Meanwhile, make the whipped salted caramel icing and the chocolate espresso icing. Place one cooled cake layer on a turntable and frost the top with about half the whipped

salted caramel icing. Repeat with the second layer. Place the third layer on top and store the cake in the freezer while you clean up and set up for the chocolate espresso icing. Giving the cake some time in the freezer at this point will set up the whipped icing between the layers, making the cake more stable and easier to frost. It helps keep everything together, especially when you're working with whipped fillings. Bring the cake from the freezer and cover the top and sides with the chocolate espresso icing.

5. Scatter the chocolate crumble over the top and then dust the top and sides of the cake with the sprinkle-nonpareil mixture.

ALMOND CAKE

I remember the first time I ever had marzipan. I was seven or eight years old and it was on my brother's bar mitzvah cake. Once I tasted it, there was no turning back. To get the flavor of the almond paste to come through the whole cake, I mix it with the sugar in the food processor; this gives it a sandy consistency.

½ pound (2 sticks) unsalted butter, plus more for greasing the pan

2 cups sugar

One 7-ounce package almond paste

2 teaspoons pure vanilla extract

4 large eggs

3 cups all-purpose flour

2 teaspoons baking powder

¼ teaspoon fine sea salt

1¾ cups whole milk (or buttermilk)

1. Have all your ingredients at room temperature. Preheat the oven to 350°F. Butter the pan of your choice or line the pan with wax paper or parchment and butter the paper.

2. With a hand mixer or a stand mixer fitted with the paddle attachment, whip the butter for 1 minute on high speed, then scrape down the sides of the bowl with a spatula.

3. In the bowl of a food processor, pulse together the sugar and the almond paste until completely combined.

4. Add the sugar mixture to the butter and beat on high speed for 2 minutes. Scrape down the sides of the bowl again.

5. With the mixer on medium-low speed, add the vanilla; then add the eggs one at a time. Scrape down the sides of the bowl midway through.

6. Combine the flour, baking powder, and sea salt in a separate bowl.

7. With the mixer on low speed, add half the flour mixture. When it's mostly incorporated, add half the milk. Add the remainder of the dry and wet ingredients, scraping down the sides of the bowl between additions. Stop mixing as soon as you have a smooth batter.

8. Pour the batter into the prepared pan and bake until the middle of the cake feels springy when you gently press your finger against it (see page 31 for approximate baking times). All ovens are different, so it's important to do the fingerprint test (see page 30) to see if the cake is done.

9. Let the cake cool completely before icing.

RAINBOW COOKIE CAKE

· ·

CAKE: **Almond Cake**

FILLING: **Store-bought strawberry jam**

GLAZE: **Chocolate Glaze**

TOPPINGS: **Pink, green, and yellow sprinkles and nonpareils**

· ·

My love of marzipan is why I love rainbow cookies, which you'll find in every Italian bakery. I've never really looked at a recipe for them, but I know they taste like marzipan.

Although the cookies are a little denser, this cake has a similar texture—but it's still light and fluffy enough to keep its integrity as a cake. Using a 3½-inch round cutter, I've made a towering mini-cake here. You can make three of these. I've matched the colors of the sprinkles to the colors of the cake layers.

More proof that anything can be a cake.

1½ recipes Almond Cake (page 104)

Pink, green, and yellow food coloring

One 13-ounce jar store-bought strawberry jam

2 recipes Chocolate Glaze (page 222)

½ cup pink, green, and yellow sprinkles and nonpareils, mixed

1. Preheat the oven to 350°F. Butter 3 quarter-sheet pans or butter the pans and then line them with wax paper or parchment and butter the paper.

2. Mix the almond cake batter according to the recipe directions and divide the batter among three bowls. Add food coloring, 1 drop at a time, to each bowl of batter until you reach the desired colors of pink, green, and yellow.

3. Pour one color of batter into each prepared pan and bake until the middle of a cake feels springy when you gently press your finger against it (see page 30), about 30 minutes.

4. Let the cakes cools completely. Once cooled, use a 3½-inch round cutter to cut two rounds from each pan.

5. Place one pink layer on a turntable and spread the top with a thin layer of jam. Repeat with a yellow and then a green layer, then repeat the sequence one more. Don't spread jam on the top layer.

6. Mix the chocolate glaze to a drippy consistency and pour it over the top of the cake. It will run down the sides to cover. Coat with the sprinkle mixture.

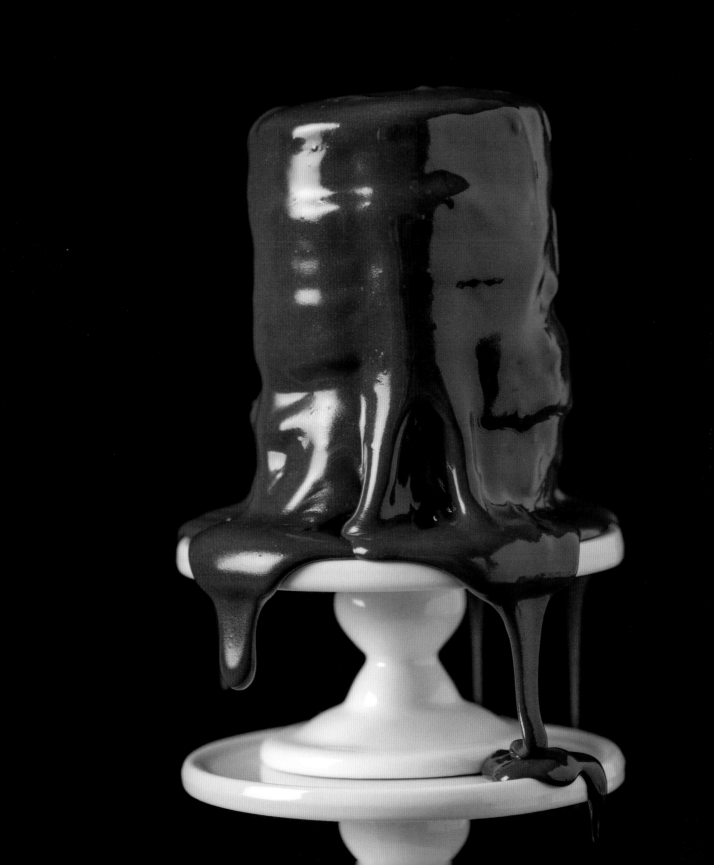

HUMMINGBIRD CAKE

This is a slightly more complicated cake, solely because of the number of ingredients. The girls in the office ordered it for someone's birthday, and I had never had it before. Fruit in cake is not usually my thing—I like a very smooth consistency. I thought I wouldn't like it, but it was delicious. I thanked them that day for bringing this cake into my life.

I liked it so much I made it a Baked by Melissa Mini of the Month. It's now an office favorite and some of my teammates are so obsessed with it they keep some in their home freezers so they can have it every day. I blend the nuts, pineapple, and coconut very fine in the food processor so the cake is not chunky.

2 to 3 ripe bananas, pureed (you want ¾ cup)

¾ cup canned crushed pineapple

½ pound (2 sticks) unsalted butter, plus more for greasing the pan

2 cups sugar

2 teaspoons pure vanilla extract

4 large eggs

⅔ cup unsweetened shredded coconut

⅔ cup finely ground pecans

I like the nuts finely ground, but if you prefer roughly chopped, go for it.

2½ cups all-purpose flour

2 teaspoons baking powder

1½ teaspoons ground cinnamon

¼ teaspoon fine sea salt

½ cup whole milk

1. Have all your ingredients at room temperature. Preheat the oven to 350°F. Butter the pan of your choice or line the pan with wax paper or parchment and butter the paper.

2. In the bowl of a food processor, puree the banana and pineapple until combined.

3. With a hand mixer or a stand mixer fitted with the paddle attachment, whip the butter for 1 minute on high speed, then scrape down the sides of the bowl with a spatula.

4. Add the sugar to the butter and beat on high speed for 2 minutes. Scrape down the sides of the bowl again.

5. With the mixer on medium-low speed, add the vanilla; then add the eggs one at a time. Scrape down the sides of the bowl midway through. Add the coconut and the pecans and mix until combined.

6. Combine the flour, baking powder, cinnamon, and sea salt in a separate bowl. Add the milk to the pureed fruit and pulse a few times to combine.

7. With the mixer on low speed, add half the flour mixture. When it's mostly incorporated, add half the milk mixture. Add the remainder of the dry and wet ingredients, scraping down the sides of the bowl between additions. Stop mixing as soon as you have a smooth batter.

8. Pour the batter into the prepared pan and bake until the middle of the cake feels springy when you gently press your finger against it (see page 31 for approximate baking times). All ovens are different, so it's important to do the fingerprint test (see page 30) to see if the cake is done.

9. Let the cake cool completely before icing.

HUMMINGBIRD CUPCAKES

CAKE: **Hummingbird Cake**
(page 112)

TOPPING: **Hummingbird Brittle**
(page 255)

ICING: **Cream Cheese Icing**
(page 185)

The Hummingbird Cupcakes are iced with Cream Cheese Icing (Cheesecake Icing would also be delicious) and topped with Hummingbird Brittle. To make the topping, I took leftover ground pecans and dried unsweetened coconut flakes, spread them in a thin layer on a half-sheet pan, and covered them with white chocolate. (It's the same method used to make the Dark Chocolate Rainbow Brittle, shown on page 255.) That's what's fun about brittle: you can use any dry shaving or topping, or sprinkles or sugar crystals, and the possibilities are endless.

PEANUT BUTTER CAKE

MMMmmm. To me, the most important part of this cake is getting peanut butter to be the star, because there's so much other stuff in it. I love plain peanut butter and use it instead of icing all the time. The Baked by Melissa Peanut Butter and Jelly Cupcake does not have icing; it has peanut butter, because the peanut butter and jelly flavor needs to shine. With this cake I had that same goal—make peanut butter the star of the show. I hope you enjoy it.

½ pound (2 sticks) unsalted butter, plus more for greasing the pan

1 cup smooth peanut butter

2 cups sugar

2 teaspoons pure vanilla extract

4 large eggs

2½ cups all-purpose flour

2 teaspoons baking powder

¼ teaspoon fine sea salt

1¾ cups whole milk (or buttermilk)

1. Have all your ingredients at room temperature. Preheat the oven to 350°F. Butter the pan of your choice or line the pan with wax paper or parchment and butter the paper.

2. With a hand mixer or a stand mixer fitted with the paddle attachment, whip the butter and the peanut butter for 1 minute on high speed, then scrape down the sides of the bowl with a spatula.

3. Add the sugar to the butter and beat on high speed for 2 minutes. Scrape down the sides of the bowl again.

4. With the mixer on medium-low speed, add the vanilla; then add the eggs one at a time. Scrape down the sides of the bowl midway through.

5. Combine the flour, baking powder, and sea salt in a separate bowl.

6. With the mixer on low speed, add half the flour mixture. When it's mostly incorporated, add half the milk. Add the remainder of the dry and wet ingredients, scraping down the sides of the bowl between additions. Stop mixing as soon as you have a smooth batter.

7. Pour the batter into the prepared pan and bake until the middle of the cake feels springy when you gently press your finger against it (see page 31 for approximate baking times). All ovens are different, so it's important to do the fingerprint test (see page 30) to see if the cake is done.

8. Let the cake cool completely before icing.

SCOTTIE'S SMASH CAKE

CAKES: **Banana Cake, Grandma Annie's Chocolate Cake, and Peanut Butter Cake**

FILLING: **Smooth peanut butter**

ICING: **Vanilla Icing**

TOPPINGS: **Rainbow sprinkles and nonpareils**

My daughter, Scottie, and her two best friends were celebrating their first birthdays at the same time as our photo shoots, so of course I had to include them in the fun. All parents want one more excuse to capture their child's first birthday. I guess that—and Pinterest—is how smash cakes became a thing.

On pages 124–125, that's Scottie in the middle, with Addison to her right and Sadie to her left. Addison's mom, Rachel, and I went to camp together and we've been very close friends since we were ten years old. We live in the same neighborhood and we both got pregnant at the same time. I met Sadie's mom, Erica, when the girls were two months old. We immediately hit it off at a lunch that Rachel had organized for all the new moms she knew in the neighborhood.

A smash cake is usually a child's very first cake. Obviously, Scottie has had cake before, but it was nice for her to have her smash cake with her besties.

In making a small cake for each of the girls, I thought about Scottie and everything that she loves to eat, so it has three different layers—banana, chocolate, and peanut butter—with real peanut butter (not icing) between them. Sadie's cake has chocolate icing, while Scottie's and Addison's cakes are decorated with vanilla icing in ombre colors.

Half recipes of at least two cake batters will make two 3½-inch smash cakes.

½ recipe Banana Cake (page 130)

½ recipe Grandma Annie's Chocolate Cake (page 89)

½ recipe Peanut Butter Cake (page 116)

1 recipe Vanilla Icing (page 161)

Pink, blue, and green food coloring

Make sure your toddler isn't allergic to peanut butter before serving this cake!

One 16-ounce jar smooth peanut butter, preferably natural, at room temperature

½ cup rainbow sprinkles and nonpareils, mixed

1. Preheat the oven to 350°F. Butter three 9 x 13-inch quarter-sheet pans or line them with wax paper or parchment and butter the paper.

2. Mix the banana, chocolate, and peanut butter cake batters according to the recipe directions. Pour into the prepared pans and bake until the middle of the cakes feel springy if you gently press your finger against them (see page 30), about 40 minutes.

3. Set the cakes aside on a rack to cool.

4. Meanwhile, make the vanilla icing. Pour half the icing into a bowl and divide the remaining half between two smaller bowls. Add 3 drops of blue food coloring for every 1 drop of green food coloring to one of the smaller bowls 1 drop at a time to achieve a teal. Add pink food coloring to one of the smaller bowls 1 drop at a time to achieve a dark pink. Add slightly less coloring to the other small bowl 1 drop at a time to achieve a paler pink.

5. Use a 3½-inch round cutter to cut one round from each cake. Place one cake layer on a rotating turntable and thickly frost the top with peanut butter; repeat with the second layer. Place the third layer and frost the entire cake with the white vanilla icing. Place the teal and pale pink icings in disposable piping bags and cut about ½ inch from the tips. Pipe one ribbon of teal icing around the base of the cake; pipe a ribbon of the pale pink around the middle. Spread the colored icing smooth using a bench scraper. Top the cake with the sprinkle mixture.

PUMPKIN SPICE CAKE

There are two variations of this cake. The Pumpkin Spice Cake (page 129, bottom right) is for people who genuinely love pumpkin; the Pumpkin Spice Latte Cake (page 129, top left) is for people who love pumpkin spice lattes. They're two different people, with two totally different palates. The true pumpkin lover likes the texture of pumpkin and that cake can be made in a loaf pan, because it's more like a bread. The pumpkin adds a certain density; you put a little bit of spice in it but you let the pumpkin be the star.

Pumpkin Spice Latte Cake has no pumpkin; I just added a little orange food coloring and pumpkin pie spice. People will say, "The pumpkin flavor is so delicious," but it's actually the spice blend they love so much.

½ pound (2 sticks) unsalted butter, plus more for greasing the pan

2 cups packed light brown sugar

2 teaspoons pure vanilla extract

4 large eggs

3 cups all-purpose flour

1 tablespoon pumpkin pie spice (see Note)

2 teaspoons baking powder

¼ teaspoon fine sea salt

½ cup whole milk (or buttermilk)

One 15-ounce can pumpkin puree (do not use pumpkin pie filling)

1. Have all your ingredients at room temperature. Preheat the oven to 350°F. Butter the pan of your choice or line the pan with wax paper or parchment and butter the paper.

2. With a hand mixer or a stand mixer fitted with the paddle attachment, whip the butter for 1 minute on high speed, then scrape down the sides of the bowl with a spatula.

3. Add the brown sugar to the butter and beat on high speed for 2 minutes. Scrape down the sides of the bowl again.

4. With the mixer on medium-low speed, add the vanilla; then add the eggs one at a time. Scrape down the sides of the bowl midway through.

5. Combine the flour, pumpkin pie spice, baking powder, and sea salt in a separate bowl. In another bowl, whisk the milk and pumpkin until blended.

6. With the mixer on low speed, add half the flour mixture. When it's mostly incorporated, add half the milk mixture. Add the remainder of the dry and wet ingredients, scraping

down the sides of the bowl between additions. Stop mixing as soon as you have a smooth batter.

7. Pour the batter into the prepared pan and bake until the middle of the cake feels springy when you gently press your finger against it (see page 31 for approximate baking times). All ovens are different, so it's important to do the fingerprint test (see page 30) to see if the cake is done.

8. Let the cake cool completely before icing.

NOTE
· ·

I use store-bought pumpkin pie spice, but if you're inspired to make your own, combine the following: 3 tablespoons ground cinnamon, 2 teaspoons ground ginger, 2 teaspoons ground nutmeg, 1½ teaspoons ground allspice, and 1 ½ teaspoons ground cloves. Store in a lidded jar.

PUMPKIN SPICE LATTE CAKE
· ·

Omit the pumpkin puree. Increase the milk to 1¾ cups and the pumpkin pie spice to 2 tablespoons. Add orange food coloring 1 drop at a time, mixing after each one, until you reach the desired color.

PUMPKIN SPICE CAKE

CAKE: **Pumpkin Spice Cake (page 126)**

FILLING: **Cheesecake Icing (page 192)**

ICING: **Cheesecake Icing (page 192)**

TOPPING: **Orange nonpareils**

PUMPKIN SPICE LATTE CAKE

CAKE: **Pumpkin Spice Latte Cake (page 127)**

FILLING: **Whipped Espresso Icing (page 205)**

ICING: **Pumpkin Spice Latte Icing (page 200)**

TOPPING: **Orange nonpareils**

Pumpkin Spice Cake (bottom right) is for people who genuinely love pumpkin; the Pumpkin Spice Latte Cake (top left) is for people who love pumpkin spice lattes. I add a little bit of spice to the Pumpkin Spice Cake, but the pumpkin is the star. It's stuffed and frosted with Cheesecake Icing. Pumpkin Spice Latte Cake has no pumpkin; I add a little orange food coloring and an extra spoonful of pumpkin pie spice, then spread Whipped Espresso Icing between the layers for a true Pumpkin Spice Latte flavor experience. The Pumpkin Spice Latte Cake is frosted with Pumpkin Spice Latte Icing. Each cake is baked in two 9-inch round pans, then sliced in half with a serrated knife to make four thin layers. Orange nonpareils decorate the edge of each cake.

BANANA CAKE

I love my mom's banana bread—specifically, banana bread with chocolate chips. When I was growing up that was one of my favorite things (along with peanut butter). So naturally we had to do a banana cupcake at Baked by Melissa. The September 2015 Mini of the Month—Peanut Butter and Banana—was inspired by my pregnancy cravings. I recommend pairing this banana cake with peanut butter, either straight from the jar or with Peanut Butter Icing (page 174), and topping it with chocolate chips. This is a great recipe for people who aren't too into sweets.

½ pound (2 sticks) unsalted butter, plus more for greasing the pan

2 cups packed light brown sugar

2 teaspoons pure vanilla extract

4 large eggs

3 cups all purpose flour

2 teaspoons baking powder

1½ teaspoons ground cinnamon

¼ teaspoon fine sea salt

6 to 7 ripe bananas, pureed (you need 2 cups)

1 cup whole milk (or buttermilk)

1. Have all your ingredients at room temperature. Preheat the oven to 350°F. Butter the pan of your choice or line the pan with wax paper or parchment and butter the paper.

2. With a hand mixer or a stand mixer fitted with the paddle attachment, whip the butter for 1 minute on high speed, then scrape down the sides of the bowl with a spatula.

3. Add the brown sugar to the butter and beat on high speed for 2 minutes. Scrape down the sides of the bowl again.

4. With the mixer on medium-low speed, add the vanilla; then add the eggs one at a time. Scrape down the edges of the bowl midway through.

5. Combine the flour, baking powder, cinnamon, and sea salt in a separate bowl. In another bowl, stir together the bananas and milk.

6. With the mixer on low speed, add half the flour mixture. When it's mostly incorporated, add half the milk mixture. Add the remainder of the dry and wet ingredients, scraping

down the sides of the bowl between additions. Stop mixing as soon as you have a smooth batter.

7. Pour the batter into the prepared pan and bake until the middle of the cake feels springy when you gently press your finger against it (see page 31 for approximate baking times). All ovens are different, so it's important to do the fingerprint test (see page 30) to see if the cake is done.

8. Let the cake cool completely before icing.

CHOCOLATE CHIP BANANA CAKE

Fold in 1 cup micro chocolate chips (see page 24) after you have mixed the batter.

HOW TO RIPEN BANANAS

If your bananas are not fully ripe, lay them on a baking sheet and bake at 300°F until the peels turn black, 20 to 30 minutes. Let them cool, then peel them and puree in a blender or food processor.

MINI BANANA CAKE LOAVES

There's no difference between my banana cake and banana bread, so you should use it as such. It's a canvas for whatever ingredients you want to add. My favorite variation is a peanut butter and Nutella swirl: Pour plain peanut butter and Nutella, about ½ cup each, into separate bowls and pop them in the microwave for a few seconds. Pour the Banana Cake (page 130) batter into the loaf pans, then add the peanut butter and the

Nutella on top. Take a skewer and swirl them around to mix the two and form a nice pattern. Other toppings shown here are (left to right) chocolate chip, plain, walnut, and blueberry. For approximate baking time, see the chart on page 31. Sprinkle the loaves with coarse sea salt after they come out of the oven.

EVERYTHING BUT THE KITCHEN SINK MUFFINS

We had some batter left over at the photo shoot from each of the different types of loaves so I made some banana muffins—giant, everything-but-the-kitchen-sink muffins, with blueberries, walnuts, chocolate chips, cinnamon, and sea salt on top.

BANANA CAKE WITH PEANUT BUTTER

CAKE: **Banana Cake**

FILLING: **Peanut butter and sliced bananas**

ICING: **Peanut butter**

TOPPING: **Chocolate chips and mixed rainbow sprinkles and nonpareils**

This cake is one of my favorites because, well, peanut butter. But the banana cake recipe in this book is also one of my favorites. I make this cake at home, too, as a loaf cake. My daughter, Scottie, loves it.

With this recipe, you can be creative without having to dirty a lot of bowls. It looks like something really decadent and over the top, but it tastes like a peanut butter and banana sandwich—the perfect ratio of peanut butter to banana.

I love plain peanut butter, and use it instead of icing all the time. It has less sugar and you can spread it right out of the jar. I also like a hint of chocolate, and the chocolate chip topping completes it for me. I make sure to get a chocolate chip in every bite.

2 recipes Banana Cake (page 130)

Two 16-ounce jars smooth peanut butter, preferably natural, at room temperature

3 bananas, sliced

½ cup chocolate chips

¼ cup rainbow sprinkles and nonpareils, mixed

1. Preheat the oven to 350°F. Butter two 13 x 18-inch half-sheet pans, then line them with wax paper or parchment and butter the paper.

2. Make the banana cakes according to the recipe directions. Pour into the prepared pans and bake until the middle of the cake feels springy when you gently press your finger against it (see page 30), about 40 minutes.

3. Set the pans on a rack and cool completely.

4. With a 6-inch round cookie cutter, cut five circles from the cakes. Place one layer on a cake stand and use an offset spatula or butter knife to spread it with peanut butter. I like to be generous with the peanut butter between the layers because I can never have enough of it, but do what you like. Place another layer on top and line the outer edge of the peanut butter with banana slices. Repeat with the third layer. Add the fourth layer and spread it with peanut butter. Top with the fifth layer, spread with peanut butter, and decorate with chocolate chips and the sprinkles mixture.

CARROT CAKE

I don't always sit around and think up ideas for cakes and concoctions on my own. A lot of times people tell me what their favorite cake is, or recount a memory from their childhood or a moment from their life, and it triggers ideas. I love having the opportunity to bring other people's memories or experiences to life through food.

There is pumpkin pie spice in this batter for a very specific reason: Peter, one of my teammates, told me about the carrot cake he made at a previous job that was so good, the staff would bake it for themselves. He said the secret was pumpkin pie spice. I'm re-creating Peter's flavor memory here and he was right—it's delicious.

If you're like me and you like a little hint of chocolate in everything, you can add ½ cup chocolate chips to this recipe. The spice and chocolate pair together really well, and when you add the crunch of nuts, it has incredible depth of flavor. It's typical to use cream cheese icing for carrot cake but if you're really looking for something new, I would recommend cheesecake icing.

½ pound (2 sticks) unsalted butter, plus more for greasing the pan

2 cups sugar

2 teaspoons pure vanilla extract

4 large eggs

2½ cups all-purpose flour

2 teaspoons baking powder

1 tablespoon pumpkin pie spice (see page 127)

¼ teaspoon fine sea salt

1¾ cups whole milk

1 teaspoon freshly squeezed lemon juice

5 to 6 carrots (about 1 pound), shredded (you want 2 cups)

1 cup chopped walnuts

1. Have all your ingredients at room temperature. Preheat the oven to 350°F. Butter the pan of your choice or line the pan with wax paper or parchment and butter the paper.

2. With a hand mixer or a stand mixer fitted with the paddle attachment, whip the butter for 1 minute on high speed, then scrape down the sides of the bowl with a spatula.

3. Add the sugar to the butter and beat on high speed for 2 minutes. Scrape down the sides of the bowl again.

4. With the mixer on medium-low speed, add the vanilla; then add the eggs one at a time. Scrape down the sides of the bowl midway through.

5. Combine the flour, baking powder, pumpkin pie spice, and sea salt in a separate bowl. In another bowl, stir together the milk, lemon juice, and shredded carrots.

6. With the mixer on low speed, add half the flour mixture. When it's mostly incorporated, add half the milk mixture. Add the remainder of the dry and wet ingredients, scraping down the sides of the bowl between additions. Stop mixing as soon as you have a nearly smooth batter (it won't be perfect because of the carrots). With a spatula, fold in the walnuts.

7. Pour the batter into the prepared pan and bake until the middle of the cake feels springy when you gently press your finger against it (see page 31 for approximate baking times). All ovens are different, so it's important to do the fingerprint test (see page 30) to see if the cake is done.

8. Let the cake cool completely before icing.

CHOCOLATE CHIP CARROT CAKE

Add ⅔ cup micro chocolate chips (see page 24) when folding in the walnuts.

PANCAKE CAKE

My dad and I used to make chocolate chip pancakes almost every Sunday morning when I was growing up. You can put fruit in yours if you want—this recipe totally works with anything you would typically add to your pancakes.

It also makes great muffins. You don't need to ice them—just top them with a pat of butter and maple syrup. Or, if you're not planning to ice the cake or top the muffins, add ⅓ cup maple syrup to the batter. (I think I ate ten of these during the photo shoot.)

You could bake pancake mix as a cake, but it would be dry and gritty. I combine store-bought pancake mix (whatever you use at home is fine) with my Classic Vanilla Cake and mix the two batters. After 10 minutes of baking, pull the pan from the oven and sprinkle the top of the cake with whatever you like to add to your pancakes—chocolate chips, blueberries, bananas. Once the batter has set a little bit, the additions won't sink to the bottom. (Bonus points if you arrange the additions in a smiley face.)

8 tablespoons (1 stick) unsalted butter, plus more for greasing the pan

1 cup sugar

1 teaspoon pure vanilla extract

2 large eggs

1½ cups all-purpose flour

1 teaspoon baking powder

Pinch of fine sea salt

¾ cup whole milk (or buttermilk)

3 tablespoons maple syrup (optional)

2 boxes store-bought pancake mix (plus required ingredients)

Your choice of chocolate chips, blueberries, or sliced bananas

1. Have all your ingredients at room temperature. Preheat the oven to 350°F. Butter the pan of your choice or line the pan with wax paper or parchment and butter the paper.

2. With a hand mixer or a stand mixer fitted with the paddle attachment, whip the butter for 1 minute on high speed, then scrape down the sides of the bowl with a spatula.

3. Add the sugar to the butter and beat on high speed for 2 minutes. Scrape down the sides of the bowl again.

4. With the mixer on medium-low speed, add the vanilla; then add the eggs one at a time. Scrape down the sides of the bowl midway through.

5. Combine the flour, baking powder, and sea salt in a separate bowl.

6. With the mixer on low speed, add half the flour mixture. When it's mostly incorporated, add half the milk. Add the remainder of the dry and wet ingredients, scraping down the sides of the bowl between additions. Stop mixing as soon as you have a smooth batter.

7. Mix the pancake batter according to the directions on the box. Add the pancake batter to the cake batter and mix on low speed until blended.

8. Pour the combined batter into the prepared pan. If you are adding chocolate chips, bake the cake for 10 minutes, then pull it from the oven and sprinkle the chocolate chips on top. Bake until the middle of the cake feels springy when you gently press your finger against it (see page 31 for approximate baking times). All ovens are different, so it's important to do the fingerprint test (see page 30) to see if the cake is done. Let the cake cool completely before icing.

ICE CREAM SANDWICHES WITH PANCAKE CAKE

. . . .

CAKE: **Pancake Cake (page 144) with chocolate chips mixed in**

TOPPINGS: **Hot fudge, maple syrup, and rainbow sprinkles**

FILLINGS: **Vanilla and chocolate ice cream**

. . . .

I love breakfast, and I love to eat breakfast for dessert. For the first three years I lived in Manhattan, I ordered a waffle with ice cream from the diner every night after dinner. A waffle with chocolate ice cream, maple syrup, and chocolate syrup on the side. It was the best thing ever. That's what I was thinking about when I made this—it's so fun and so delicious and allows you to eat breakfast for dessert.

To make ice cream sandwiches, make pancake cake, using chocolate chips as the mix-in, and bake in a half-sheet pan. Use 3½-inch round cutters to cut out the finished cakes. Cut out as many as the pan allows. The harder the ice cream the better—you want it to keep its shape until it's served. Scoop out the ice cream and put it on a sheet pan and put it back in the freezer so it's not melty when you assemble the sandwiches. These are great for a party—you could set up a buffet with different ice cream flavors and toppings and let everyone make their own.

You could also make this cake in a waffle iron (see page 29) for actual waffles with ice cream. I recently surprised my whole office with cake waffles one morning, topped with maple syrup, and everyone loved them!

COCONUT CAKE

As with the Strawberry Cake (page 55), which uses fresh strawberries, I knew I'd want to replace part of the milk in this Coconut Cake recipe with something that would give me a natural, fresh coconut flavor. I ended up using Coco Lopez cream of coconut, which is a common ingredient in piña coladas. That's a very nostalgic flavor for me, bringing to mind family vacations to Aruba, where I'd order virgin versions of the cocktail. I don't like to use extracts, but there is coconut extract in this cake. It doesn't taste artificial, and gives an extra pop of coconut flavor.

The shredded coconut adds a bit of texture to the cake, which comes out super fluffy. The Coco Lopez also helps with that. I love coconut because of this cake.

½ pound (2 sticks) unsalted butter, plus more for greasing the pan

2 cups sugar

2 teaspoons pure vanilla extract

4 large eggs

3 cups all-purpose flour

2 teaspoons baking powder

¼ teaspoon fine sea salt

1½ cups whole milk

½ cup Coco Lopez cream of coconut

2 teaspoons coconut extract

1 cup unsweetened shredded coconut

1. Have all your ingredients at room temperature. Preheat the oven to 350°F. Butter the pan of your choice or line the pan with wax paper or parchment and butter the paper.

2. With a hand mixer or a stand mixer fitted with the paddle attachment, whip the butter for 1 minute on high speed, then scrape down the sides of the bowl with a spatula.

3. Add the sugar to the butter and beat on high speed for 2 minutes. Scrape down the sides of the bowl again.

4. With the mixer on medium-low speed, add the vanilla; then add the eggs one at a time. Scrape down the sides of the bowl midway through.

5. Combine the flour, baking powder, and sea salt in a separate bowl. In another bowl, combine the milk, cream of coconut, and coconut extract.

6. With the mixer on low speed, add half the flour mixture. When it's mostly incorporated, add half the milk mixture. Add the remainder of the dry and wet ingredients, scraping

down the sides of the bowl between additions. Stop mixing as soon as you have a smooth batter. Stir in the shredded coconut.

7. Pour the batter into the prepared pan and bake until the middle of the cake feels springy when you gently press your finger against it (see page 31 for approximate baking times). All ovens are different, so it's important to do the fingerprint test (see page 30) to see if the cake is done.

8. Let the cake cool completely before icing.

THE COCONUT CAKE

CAKE: **Coconut Cake**

FILLING: **Coconut Icing**

ICING: **Coconut Icing**

TOPPING: **Unsweetened shredded coconut and coconut flakes**

This cake is like a party in your mouth. The cake itself is very fluffy because of the coconut cream. It's all about coconut, with coconut icing and real coconut flakes covering the entire cake. I wasn't a fan of coconut when I was growing up, but I've learned to love it.

2 recipes Coconut Cake (page 148)

2 recipes Coconut Icing (page 203)

1 cup unsweetened shredded coconut

1 cup unsweetened coconut flakes

1. Preheat the oven to 350°F. Butter two 13 x 18-inch half-sheet pans, then line it with wax paper or parchment and butter the paper.

2. Mix the cake batter according to the recipe directions. Pour into the prepared pan and bake until the middle of the cake feels springy when you gently press your finger against it (see page 30), about 40 minutes.

3. Set the pan on a rack to cool completely. Using a 10-inch round cutter, cut 3 round layers from the sheet cake.

4. Meanwhile, make the coconut icing according to the recipe instructions.

5. Place one cake layer on a turntable and frost the top with about a quarter of the icing; repeat with the second layer. Place the top layer and frost the entire cake with the remainder of the coconut icing.

6. Cover the top of the cake with the coconut shreds and flakes, and press them lightly into the sides.

CORNBREAD CAKE

I have this vivid memory of going to the Pancake House in Ridgewood, New Jersey, when I was growing up. There's always a line around the corner to get in (still!) and they serve pancakes that are the size of the plate. Even better than the pancakes (and I'm a pancake person) is their cornbread. It has chocolate chips and it comes to the table warm; it's so good.

At Baked by Melissa, I create flavors that evoke the holidays throughout the year. For Thanksgiving 2014, I made our first cornbread cupcake, inspired by so many meals at the Pancake House. I replace three-quarters of the flour in my basic cake recipe with cornmeal, which gives you the taste and the texture of cornbread, while keeping that sweet cake vibe. Chocolate chips are optional.

½ pound (2 sticks) unsalted butter, plus more for greasing the pan

2 cups sugar

2 teaspoons pure vanilla extract

4 large eggs

1 cup all-purpose flour

2 cups cornmeal

2 teaspoons baking powder

¼ teaspoon fine sea salt

1¾ cups whole milk (or buttermilk)

½ cup micro chocolate chips (optional; page 24)

1. Have all your ingredients at room temperature. Preheat the oven to 350°F. Butter the pan of your choice or line the pan with wax paper or parchment and butter the paper.

2. With a hand mixer or a stand mixer fitted with the paddle attachment, whip the butter for 1 minute on high speed, then scrape down the sides of the bowl with a spatula.

3. Add the sugar to the butter and beat on high speed for 2 minutes. Scrape down the sides of the bowl again.

4. With the mixer on medium-low speed, add the vanilla; then add the eggs one at a time. Scrape down the sides of the bowl midway through.

5. Combine the flour, cornmeal, baking powder, and sea salt in a separate bowl.

6. With the mixer on low speed, add half the flour mixture. When it's mostly incorporated, add half the milk. Add the remainder of the dry and wet ingredients, scraping down the sides of the bowl between additions. Stop mixing as soon as you have a smooth batter.

7. Pour the batter into the prepared pan. If you are adding chocolate chips, bake the cake for 5 minutes, then pull it from the oven and sprinkle the chocolate chips on top. Return the cake to the oven and bake until the middle of the cake feels springy when you gently press your finger against it (see page 31 for approximate baking times). All ovens are different, so it's important to do the fingerprint test (see page 30) to see if the cake is done.

RED VELVET CAKE

This is one of the most popular flavors at Baked by Melissa—we use it in cupcakes, in gluten-free cakes, and in macarons. This recipe has a substantial amount of cocoa and if you close your eyes, you can taste it. I would recommend chocolate icing—that's how I like to eat my red velvet cake—or it goes great with chocolate cheesecake icing.

½ pound (2 sticks) unsalted butter, plus more for greasing the pan

2 cups sugar

2 teaspoons pure vanilla extract

4 large eggs

3 cups all-purpose flour

3 tablespoons unsweetened cocoa powder

2 teaspoons baking powder

¼ teaspoon fine sea salt

1¾ cups whole milk

1 tablespoon red food coloring

1. Have all your ingredients at room temperature. Preheat the oven to 350°F. Butter the pan of your choice or line the pan with wax paper or parchment and butter the paper.

2. With a hand mixer or a stand mixer fitted with the paddle attachment, whip the butter for 1 minute on high speed, then scrape down the sides of the bowl with a spatula.

3. Add the sugar to the butter and beat on high speed for 2 minutes. Scrape down the sides of the bowl again.

4. With the mixer on medium-low speed, add the vanilla; then add the eggs one at a time. Scrape down the sides of the bowl midway through.

5. Combine the flour, cocoa powder, baking powder, and sea salt in a separate bowl.

6. With the mixer on low speed, add half the flour mixture. When it's mostly incorporated, add half the milk. Add the remainder of the dry and wet ingredients, scraping down the sides of the bowl between additions. Stop mixing as soon as you have a smooth batter. Add the food coloring and beat until incorporated.

7. Pour the batter into the prepared pan and bake until the middle of the cake feels springy when you gently press your finger against it (see page 31 for approximate baking times). All ovens are different, so it's important to do the fingerprint test (see page 30) to see if the cake is done.

8. Let the cake cool completely before icing.

MINT LEAF CAKE

I'm not one for peppermint or that bottled mint extract, but I do love fresh mint. It's not easy to get the fresh mint flavor into a cake, so I combined the mint leaves and sugar in the food processor. This keeps the integrity of the leaf and lets the flavor shine through.

2 cups sugar

⅓ cup packed fresh mint leaves

½ pound (2 sticks) unsalted butter, plus more for greasing the pan

2 teaspoons pure vanilla extract

4 large eggs

3 cups all-purpose flour

2 teaspoons baking powder

¼ teaspoon fine sea salt

1¾ cups whole milk

1. Have all your ingredients at room temperature. With a hand mixer or a food processor, combine the sugar and mint leaves and process until the leaves are completely incorporated.

2. Preheat the oven to 350°F. Butter the pan of your choice or line the pan with wax paper or parchment and butter the paper.

3. With a hand mixer or a stand mixer fitted with the paddle attachment, whip the butter for 1 minute on high speed, then scrape down the sides of the bowl with a spatula.

4. Add the sugar-mint mixture to the butter and beat on high speed for 2 minutes. Scrape down the sides of the bowl again.

5. With the mixer on medium-low speed, add the vanilla; then add the eggs one at a time. Scrape down the sides of the bowl midway through.

6. Combine the flour, baking powder, and sea salt in a separate bowl.

7. With the mixer on low speed, add half the flour mixture. When it's mostly incorporated, add half the milk. Add the remainder of the dry and wet ingredients, scraping down the sides of the bowl between additions. Stop mixing as soon as you have a smooth batter.

8. Pour the batter into the prepared pan and bake until the middle of the cake feels springy when you gently press your finger against it (see page 31 for approximate baking times). All ovens are different, so it's important to do the fingerprint test (see page 30) to see if the cake is done. Let the cake cool completely before icing.

ICINGS
AND
FILLINGS

Icing complements cake. Like chocolate to peanut butter or peanut butter to jelly, it can transform a plain cake into something else entirely.

When I work with icings (or glazes) my goal is to enhance the flavor of the cake and give you more of an experience, to bring new flavors into the mix, often ones that take you back to your childhood. For example, the Baked by Melissa Cookies and Cream Cupcakes are chocolate cake paired with cookies and cream stuffing and vanilla icing. They're a perfect balance of flavors that makes you think you're eating an Oreo, or cookies and cream ice cream.

My icings go beyond the expected. I've included a recipe here for cream cheese icing, because it's a classic, but I recommend going with cheesecake icing. It gives you the opportunity to have cheesecake *and* cake, and you don't have to bake the cheesecake. This section offers you even more of an opportunity to be creative because you can choose which icing(s) to use on your base cake. Depending on what icing you use, it will either enhance or contrast with the base cake flavor. For example, a peanut butter cake with peanut butter icing is great for peanut butter lovers, but if you're like me and you like peanut butter and chocolate, that chocolate icing is just as important to the flavor experience as the peanut butter. And of course, I always recommend sprinkling any cake with coarse sea salt.

You'll notice that almost all of my icings contain a touch of salt as well, and there's a good reason for that. It's necessary to bring out the flavor, tamp down the sweet a little bit, and leave you with that dance on your tongue at the very end.

While my cakes are about re-creating memories of the past, these icings are all about innovation.

FOR A SILKIER ICING
. . . .
Add room-temperature whole milk 1 tablespoon at a time to get a more spreadable consistency.

ICING YIELDS

Each icing recipe will make 3¾ cups—enough to frost two 9-inch cakes with four layers, one sheet cake, 24 regular size cupcakes, or 48 mini cupcakes.

Each whipped icing recipe will make 4½ cups—enough to frost two 9-inch cakes with four layers, one sheet cake, 24 regular size cupcakes, or 48 mini cupcakes.

VANILLA ICING

Just like my Classic Vanilla Cake (page 34), this icing is the perfect canvas to which any flavor can be added. It has just the right amount of sweetness and vanilla flavor, and a lot of body, so it holds up well.

½ pound (2 sticks) unsalted butter, at room temperature

1 teaspoon pure vanilla extract

3¾ cups confectioners' sugar

¼ teaspoon fine sea salt

1. With a hand mixer or a stand mixer fitted with the whisk attachment, whip the butter on high speed for 1 minute. Add the vanilla and whip just to incorporate.

2. In a separate bowl, mix the sugar and salt. With the mixer on low speed (otherwise you'll be covered in confectioners' sugar), add the sugar 1 cup at a time, until completely incorporated. Scrape down the sides of the bowl between additions. Whip on high speed for 3 minutes, until light and fluffy.

STUFFING CUPCAKES

To stuff a cupcake, fill a pastry bag (I like the disposable ones) with the filling and literally puncture a hole in the top of the cake. Squeeze the pastry bag until the cupcake plumps up a little bit, but stop just before it cracks. You may need to practice a few times and even break one open to see how you did. (Then you get to eat the practice cupcakes.) You could also cut a hole from the top of the cake and slightly press in the cake around the hole to make it a little denser around the filling. I use that technique for gooier fillings, like Fluff (see page 95), because that really needs a home inside the cake. But a filling like the cookie dough icing is dense enough to push the cake out of the way and stay put.

To re-create the marble icing shown in this section, combine a scoop each of chocolate, vanilla, and strawberry icing in a disposable pastry bag for a Neapolitan swirl, squeeze until all three colors come out together, and pipe onto the cupcake.

COOKIES AND CREAM CUPCAKE

. . . .

CAKE: **Grandma Annie's Chocolate Cake**

FILLING: **Cookies and Cream Icing**

ICING: **Cookies and Cream Icing**

TOPPINGS: **Oreo Crumble and Oreo cookies**

. . . .

This cupcake is based on one of our Baked by Melissa OG (Original Greats) flavors: Cookies and Cream. I love cookies and cream ice cream, and this cake gives you that same perfect flavor balance that makes you think of an Oreo cookie.

1 recipe Grandma Annie's Chocolate Cake (page 89)

1 recipe Cookies and Cream Icing (page 176)

1 recipe Vanilla Icing (page 161)

1 recipe Oreo Crumble (page 242)

1. Preheat the oven to 350°F. Butter the wells of a 24-count mini cupcake pan, or line them with mini paper baking liners.

2. Mix the chocolate cake batter according to the recipe directions and pour the batter into the cupcake wells. Bake until the middles of the cupcakes feel springy when you gently press your finger against them (see page 30), about 30 minutes.

3. Set the cupcakes aside to cool completely.

4. Meanwhile, make the cookies and cream icing and the vanilla icing.

5. Fill a disposable pastry bag with cookies and cream icing and snip the tip of the bag about ½ inch from the end. Puncture a hole in the top of a cupcake with the tip of the pastry bag and slowly squeeze the bag to fill the cupcake. The cupcake will plump a bit, but do not fill it so much that it breaks. Fill a second pastry bag with the vanilla icing and top off each cupcake with vanilla icing. Repeat with the remaining cupcakes.

6. Sprinkle the top of each cupcake with the Oreo Crumble.

COOKIES AND CREAM CAKE

CAKE: **Grandma Annie's Chocolate Cake (page 89)**

FILLING: **Cookies and Cream Icing (page 176)**

You can use chocolate chip cookie dough as a filling, too.

ICING: **Vanilla Icing (page 161)**

GLAZE: **Marshmallow Fluff Glaze (page 232)**

TOPPINGS: **Oreo Crumble (page 242) and Oreo cookies**

It was so much fun to translate the cookies and cream cupcake into three layers—and the result is absolutely delicious. The cake is topped with Marshmallow Fluff that's thinned with a little milk to make a glaze, stuffed with cookies and cream icing, and topped with vanilla icing, and then—of course—Oreo crumble and cookie pieces.

CHOCOLATE ICING

I'm a chocolate lover, so this is one of my favorite icings. It's rich in flavor, not overly sweet, and the chocolate flavor shines.

½ pound (2 sticks) unsalted butter

1 teaspoon pure vanilla extract

3¾ cups confectioners' sugar

1 cup unsweetened cocoa powder

¼ teaspoon fine sea salt

½ cup heavy cream

1. Have all your ingredients at room temperature.

2. With a hand mixer or a stand mixer fitted with the whisk attachment, whip the butter on high speed for 1 minute. Add the vanilla extract and whip just to incorporate.

3. In a separate bowl, mix the confectioners' sugar, cocoa, and salt. With the mixer on low speed (otherwise you'll be covered in confectioners' sugar), add the sugar-cocoa mixture 1 cup at a time, until completely incorporated. Scrape down the sides of the bowl between additions. Whip on high speed for 2 minutes, until light and fluffy. Add the cream and whip on high speed for 2 minutes more.

CLASSIC BIRTHDAY CAKE

CAKE: **Classic Vanilla Cake (page 34)**

FILLING: **Chocolate Icing (page 168)**

ICING: **Chocolate Icing (page 168)**

TOPPINGS: **Rainbow sprinkles and nonpareils**

Classic Vanilla Cake with Chocolate Icing and lots of rainbow sprinkles. To me, that's birthday cake, especially when you add a sparkler.

DOUGHNUT ICING

Yes, it really does taste like doughnuts. Pair this icing with vanilla or doughnut cake and you'll shock your taste buds into thinking you've just taken a bite of a doughnut.

½ pound (2 sticks) unsalted butter, at room temperature

1 teaspoon pure vanilla extract

2 cups confectioners' sugar

½ teaspoon mace

½ teaspoon fine sea salt

1. With a hand mixer or a stand mixer fitted with the whisk attachment, whip the butter on high speed for 2 minutes. Add the vanilla and whip just to incorporate.

2. With the mixer on low speed, gradually add the confectioners' sugar, 1 cup at a time, then the mace and salt, mixing until completely incorporated. Scrape down the sides of the bowl, then whip on high speed for 2 minutes more.

CINNAMON ICING

This icing pairs well with many of the cake recipes. Try it with Classic Vanilla Cake (page 34) or Brown Sugar Cake (page 50) for a subtle and sophisticated flavor, or pair it with Grandma Annie's Chocolate Cake (page 89) and Chocolate Crumble (page 243) for a modern-day babka!

½ pound (2 sticks) unsalted butter, at room temperature

1 teaspoon pure vanilla extract

2 cups confectioners' sugar

1 tablespoon ground cinnamon

1 teaspoon fine sea salt

1. With a hand mixer or a stand mixer fitted with the whisk attachment, whip the butter on high speed for 2 minutes. Add the vanilla and whip just to incorporate.

2. With the mixer on low speed, gradually add the confectioners' sugar, 1 cup at a time, then the cinnamon and salt, mixing until completely incorporated. Scrape down the sides of the bowl, then whip on high speed for 2 minutes more.

STRAWBERRY ICING

This icing reminds me of strawberry ice cream.

½ pound (2 sticks) unsalted butter, at room temperature

1 teaspoon pure vanilla extract

3 cups confectioners' sugar

½ teaspoon fine sea salt

6 tablespoons strawberry puree (see Note, page 53)

1. With a hand mixer or a stand mixer fitted with the whisk attachment, whip the butter on high speed for 1 minute. Add the vanilla extract and whip just to incorporate.

2. With the mixer on low speed, gradually add the confectioners' sugar, 1 cup at a time, and mix until completely incorporated. Scrape down the sides of the bowl, add the salt, and whip on high speed for 3 minutes more. With a spatula, fold in the strawberry puree just until combined.

LEMON ICING

Like my Lemon Cake (page 56), this icing is light and refreshing.

½ pound (2 sticks) unsalted butter, at room temperature

½ teaspoon grated lemon zest

1 tablespoon freshly squeezed lemon juice

3¾ cups confectioners' sugar

½ teaspoon fine sea salt

1. With a hand mixer or a stand mixer fitted with the whisk attachment, whip the butter on high speed for 2 minutes. Add the lemon zest and juice and whip just to incorporate.

2. With the mixer on low speed, gradually add the confectioners' sugar, 1 cup at a time, and mix until completely incorporated. Scrape down the sides of the bowl, add the salt, and whip on high speed for 2 minutes more.

PEANUT BUTTER ICING

This is the only peanut butter icing you should ever use. It's packed with peanut butter flavor for all of my true peanut butter lovers.

½ pound (2 sticks) unsalted butter, at room temperature

1¼ cups smooth peanut butter, at room temperature

1 teaspoon pure vanilla extract

2 cups confectioners' sugar

½ teaspoon fine sea salt

1. With a hand mixer or a stand mixer fitted with the whisk attachment, whip the butter and peanut butter on high speed for 2 minutes. Add the vanilla and whip just to incorporate.

2. Combine the sugar and salt. With the mixer on low speed (otherwise you'll be covered in confectioners' sugar), add the mixture 1 cup at a time, until completely incorporated. Scrape down the sides of the bowl between additions. Whip on high speed for 2 minutes, until light and fluffy.

PEANUT BUTTER CINNAMON ICING

Add 1 tablespoon ground cinnamon to the sugar mixture.

PEANUT BUTTER CHOCOLATE ICING

Reduce the peanut butter to 1 cup and add ½ cup unsweetened cocoa powder to the sugar mixture.

SUGAR COOKIE DOUGH ICING

I love cookie dough and have never understood why it can't be an icing too. This is not as sweet as the standard icing—it's just fun and it makes you feel like you're eating cookies with your cake.

½ pound (2 sticks) unsalted butter, at room temperature

2 teaspoons pure vanilla extract

1⅓ cups granulated sugar

½ teaspoon fine sea salt

¾ cup heavy cream, at room temperature

1¼ cups all-purpose flour

1. With a hand mixer or a stand mixer fitted with the whisk attachment, whip the butter on high speed for 1 minute. Add the vanilla and whip just to incorporate.

2. With the mixer on low speed, add the sugar and salt and whip until completely incorporated. Scrape down the sides of the bowl.

3. Add the cream and whip for 1 minute. Gradually add the flour and whip just until incorporated, scraping down the sides of the bowl one last time.

COOKIES AND CREAM ICING

Cookies and cream is one of my favorite ice cream flavors. It reminds me of summers spent at Lake George with my family and today, when I walk into an ice cream parlor, it's the first flavor I look for. I love this icing with Grandma Annie's Chocolate Cake (page 89).

Crush the cookies in a food processor or in a plastic bag with a rolling pin.

½ pound (2 sticks) unsalted butter, at room temperature

1 teaspoon pure vanilla extract

3¾ cups confectioners' sugar

½ teaspoon fine sea salt

¾ cup Oreo Crumble (page 242)

¼ cup heavy cream, at room temperature

1. With a hand mixer or a stand mixer fitted with the whisk attachment, whip the butter on high speed for 1 minute. Add the vanilla and whip just to incorporate.

2. With the mixer on low speed, gradually add the confectioners' sugar, 1 cup at a time, until completely incorporated. Scrape down the sides of the bowl between additions.

3. Add the salt and Oreo crumble and whip on high speed for 3 minutes, until light and fluffy.

4. With the mixer on low speed, add the cream a little at a time, stopping when you reach the preferred consistency.

CHOCOLATE COOKIES AND CREAM ICING

Add ½ cup unsweetened cocoa powder.

ESPRESSO ICING

I use espresso instead of coffee for a richer flavor. If you don't have an espresso machine, just head to your local coffee shop and buy a cup.

½ pound (2 sticks) unsalted butter, at room temperature

1 teaspoon pure vanilla extract

¼ cup brewed espresso, at room temperature

3¾ cups confectioners' sugar

½ teaspoon fine sea salt

1. With a hand mixer or a stand mixer fitted with the whisk attachment, whip the butter on high speed for 1 minute. Add the vanilla and espresso and whip just to incorporate.

2. With the mixer on low speed, gradually add the confectioners' sugar, 1 cup at a time, until completely incorporated. Scrape down the sides of the bowl between additions.

3. Add the salt and whip on high speed for 3 minutes, until light and fluffy.

CHOCOLATE ESPRESSO ICING

. . . .

Add ½ cup unsweetened cocoa powder.

CHOCOLATE CHIP COOKIE DOUGH ICING

This is best used to stuff cupcakes and spread between the layers of your cakes.

½ pound (2 sticks) unsalted butter

1½ cups packed light brown sugar

2 teaspoons pure vanilla extract

1½ cups all-purpose flour

½ teaspoon fine sea salt

½ cup heavy cream, at room temperature

½ cup micro chocolate chips (see page 24)

1. Have all your ingredients at room temperature.

2. With a hand mixer or a stand mixer fitted with the whisk attachment, whip the butter on high speed for 2 minutes. Add the brown sugar and vanilla and whip just to incorporate.

3. In a separate bowl, combine the flour and salt. With the mixer on low speed, gradually add the flour mixture. Add the cream and, with the mixer on high speed, whip for 30 seconds more. Scrape down the sides of the bowl and with a spatula fold in the chocolate chips.

I used the cookie dough icing between layers here!

THE DOUBLE COOKIE CAKE

CAKE: **Grandma Annie's Chocolate Cake**

FILLING: **Chocolate Chip Cookie Dough Icing**

ICING: **Cookies and Cream Icing**

TOPPINGS: **Chocolate chip cookie dough, Oreo cookies, rainbow sprinkles, Oreo Crumble**

This chocolate cake is stuffed with Chocolate Chip Cookie Dough Icing and frosted with Cookies and Cream Icing. Scoops of chocolate chip cookie dough and Oreo cookies decorate the top, with rainbow sprinkles and Oreo cookie crumble added as a finishing touch.

1 recipe Grandma Annie's Chocolate Cake (page 89)

1 recipe Chocolate Chip Cookie Dough Icing (page 178)

1 recipe Cookies and Cream Icing (page 176)

One 16.5-ounce package store-bought chocolate chip cookie dough

1 sleeve Oreo cookies, broken in half

½ cup rainbow sprinkles

Oreo Crumble (page 242)

1. Preheat the oven to 350°F. Butter a 13 x 18-inch half-sheet pan, then line the pan with wax paper or parchment and butter the paper.

2. Mix the chocolate cake batter according to the recipe directions. Pour into the prepared pan and bake until the middle of the cake feels springy when you gently press your finger against it (see page 30), about 40 minutes. Set the cake aside to cool completely. Use a 6-inch round cutter to cut three layers from the pan.

3. Meanwhile, make the cookie dough icing and cookies and cream icing. Place one cake layer on a turntable and frost the top with about half the cookie dough icing; repeat with the second layer. Place the top layer and frost the entire cake with the cookies and cream icing.

4. Top the cake with a ring of alternating chunks of cookie dough and Oreo cookie halves. Decorate the top and the sides with sprinkles and press the Oreo crumble into the cake along the bottom. Serve with a big glass of cold milk.

SNICKERDOODLE ICING

One more favorite flavor from my childhood cookie jar.

½ pound (2 sticks) unsalted butter

2 teaspoons pure vanilla extract

1⅓ cups granulated sugar

1 tablespoon ground cinnamon

½ teaspoon fine sea salt

¾ cup heavy cream, at room temperature

1¼ cups all-purpose flour

1. Have all your ingredients at room temperature.

2. With a hand mixer or a stand mixer fitted with the whisk attachment, whip the butter on high speed for 1 minute. Add the vanilla and whip just to incorporate.

3. With the mixer on low speed, add the sugar, cinnamon, and salt and mix until completely incorporated. Scrape down the sides of the bowl between additions.

4. Add the heavy cream and whip for 1 minute. Gradually add the flour and whip just until incorporated, scraping down the sides of the bowl one last time.

DULCE DE LECHE ICING

With icing, as with cake, it's all about the ratio of the flavor that's added to the base recipe. This salted caramel icing is off the chain, with a perfect salty-sweet combination.

½ pound (2 sticks) unsalted butter, at room temperature

1 cup store-bought dulce de leche (see Note, page 83)

1 teaspoon pure vanilla extract

2 cups confectioners' sugar

1 teaspoon fine sea salt

1. With a hand mixer or a stand mixer fitted with the whisk attachment, whip the butter and dulce de leche on high speed for 2 minutes. Add the vanilla and whip just to incorporate.

2. With the mixer on low speed, gradually add the confectioners' sugar, 1 cup at a time, and mix until completely incorporated. Scrape down the sides of the bowl, add the salt, and whip on high speed for 2 minutes more.

SALTED CARAMEL ICING

Increase the fine sea salt to 2 teaspoons.

CREAM CHEESE ICING

This is my version of the classic icing. Don't even think of using low-fat cream cheese.

½ pound (2 sticks) unsalted butter, at room temperature

One 8-ounce package Philadelphia full-fat cream cheese, at room temperature

The only way to go!

1 teaspoon pure vanilla extract

3¾ cups confectioners' sugar

½ teaspoon fine sea salt

1. With a hand mixer or a stand mixer fitted with the whisk attachment, whip the butter and cream cheese on high speed for 2 minutes. Add the vanilla and whip just to incorporate.

2. With the mixer on low speed, gradually add the confectioners' sugar, 1 cup at a time, then the salt, mixing until completely incorporated. Scrape down the sides of the bowl, then whip on high speed for 2 minutes more.

PEANUT BUTTER CREAM CHEESE ICING

Add 1 cup smooth peanut butter, at room temperature, and reduce the confectioners' sugar to 2 cups.

CHOCOLATE CREAM CHEESE ICING

Add 1 cup unsweetened cocoa powder and reduce the confectioners' sugar to 2 cups.

HOT COCOA ICING

Pair this icing with the Hot Cocoa Cake (page 68) and you'll have the ultimate hot cocoa lover's experience. I could eat this icing for breakfast, lunch, and dinner. It is that good.

½ pound (2 sticks) unsalted butter, at room temperature

1 teaspoon pure vanilla extract

2 cups confectioners' sugar

1½ cups hot cocoa mix

¼ teaspoon fine sea salt

1. With a hand mixer or a stand mixer fitted with the whisk attachment, whip the butter on high speed for 1 minute. Add the vanilla and whip just to incorporate.

2. With the mixer on low speed, gradually add the confectioners' sugar and cocoa mix, 1 cup at a time, until completely incorporated. Scrape down the sides of the bowl between additions.

3. Add the salt and whip on high speed for 3 minutes, until light and fluffy.

HOT COCOA CUPCAKES

Just as gooey and good as the Hot Cocoa Cake (page 71), these cupcakes are made with Grandma Annie's Chocolate Cake (page 89), stuffed with Marshmallow Fluff Glaze, iced with Hot Cocoa Icing (facing page), and topped with Marshmallow Fluff Glaze (page 232) and Hot Cocoa Glaze (page 231).

MATCHA ICING

With the beautiful green color and subtle flavor of matcha tea, this is a sophisticated icing that pairs well with Classic Vanilla Cake (page 34) as well as Matcha Cake (page 84).

½ pound (2 sticks) unsalted butter, at room temperature

1 teaspoon pure vanilla extract

3¾ cups confectioners' sugar

2 tablespoons matcha green tea powder

¼ teaspoon fine sea salt

1 drop green food coloring

1. With a hand mixer or a stand mixer fitted with the whisk attachment, whip the butter on high speed for 1 minute. Add the vanilla and whip just to incorporate.

2. With the mixer on low speed, gradually add the confectioners' sugar and matcha powder, 1 cup at a time, until completely incorporated. Scrape down the sides of the bowl between additions.

3. Add the salt and the food coloring and whip on high speed for 3 minutes, until light and fluffy.

MAPLE ICING

Be sure to use real maple syrup (I like Grade A very dark) for a true maple flavor that's rich, complex, and not too sweet. This works well on Pancake Cake (page 144).

½ pound (2 sticks) unsalted butter, at room temperature

½ cup real maple syrup, at room temperature

1 teaspoon pure vanilla extract

3¾ cups confectioners' sugar

¼ teaspoon fine sea salt

1. With a hand mixer or a stand mixer fitted with the whisk attachment, whip the butter on high speed for 1 minute. Add the maple syrup and vanilla and whip just to incorporate.

2. With the mixer on low speed, gradually add the confectioners' sugar, 1 cup at a time, until completely incorporated. Scrape down the sides of the bowl between additions.

3. Add the salt and whip on high speed for 3 minutes, until light and fluffy.

MARSHMALLOW ICING

½ pound (2 sticks) unsalted butter, at room temperature

2 cups Marshmallow Fluff

1 teaspoon pure vanilla extract

3¾ cups confectioners' sugar

¼ teaspoon fine sea salt

1. With a hand mixer or a stand mixer fitted with the whisk attachment, whip the butter on high speed for 1 minute. Add the Marshmallow Fluff and vanilla and whip just to incorporate.

2. With the mixer on low speed, gradually add the confectioners' sugar, 1 cup at a time, until completely incorporated. Scrape down the sides of the bowl between additions.

3. Add the salt and whip on high speed for 3 minutes, until light and fluffy.

NUTELLA ICING

½ pound (2 sticks) unsalted butter

1 teaspoon pure vanilla extract

3¾ cups confectioners' sugar

¼ teaspoon fine sea salt

½ cup Nutella

¼ cup heavy cream, at room temperature

1. Have all your ingredients at room temperature.

2. With a hand mixer or a stand mixer fitted with the whisk attachment, whip the butter on high speed for 1 minute. Add the vanilla and whip just to incorporate.

3. With the mixer on low speed, gradually add the confectioners' sugar, 1 cup at a time, until completely incorporated. Scrape down the sides of the bowl between additions.

4. Add the salt, Nutella, and heavy cream and whip on high speed for 3 minutes, until light and fluffy.

COFFEE CARAMEL ICING

This icing gets its rich color and flavor from the mixture of dulce de leche and brewed espresso. If you don't have an espresso machine at home, pick up an espresso at your local coffee shop.

½ pound (2 sticks) unsalted butter

1 cup store-bought dulce de leche (see Note, page 83)

1 teaspoon pure vanilla extract

2 cups confectioners' sugar

1 teaspoon fine sea salt

¼ cup brewed espresso

¼ cup all-purpose flour

1. Have all your ingredients at room temperature.

2. With a hand mixer or a stand mixer fitted with the whisk attachment, whip the butter and dulce de leche on high speed for 2 minutes. Add the vanilla and whip just to incorporate.

3. With the mixer on low speed, gradually add the confectioners' sugar, 1 cup at a time, and mix until completely incorporated, scraping down the sides of the bowl between additions. Add the salt and whip on high speed for 2 minutes more.

4. Add the espresso, mixing until completely incorporated, then the flour, and whip just to combine.

CHEESECAKE ICING

This icing is something special. To create the cheesecake experience in icing form, I doubled up on the cream cheese and added some lemon, because when you're dealing with a lot of cream cheese you need to brighten the flavor. I also use less sugar and butter than usual for an icing to help the cheesecake texture come through. The butter and cream cheese *must* be at room temperature.

8 tablespoons (1 stick) unsalted butter, at room temperature

Two 8-ounce packages Philadelphia full-fat cream cheese, at room temperature → *The only way to go!*

1 teaspoon pure vanilla extract

1 teaspoon freshly squeezed lemon juice

1 cup confectioners' sugar

½ teaspoon fine sea salt

1. With a hand mixer or a stand mixer fitted with the whisk attachment, whip the butter and cream cheese on high speed for 2 minutes. Add the vanilla and lemon juice and whip just to incorporate.

2. With the mixer on low speed, gradually add the confectioners' sugar, 1 cup at a time, and mix until completely incorporated, scraping down the sides of the bowl between additions. Add the salt and whip on high speed for 2 minutes more.

STRAWBERRY CHEESECAKE ICING

Add ¼ cup plus 2 tablespoons strawberry puree (see page 53).

CINNAMON CHEESECAKE ICING

Add 1 tablespoon ground cinnamon.

PEANUT BUTTER CHEESECAKE ICING

Add ½ cup smooth peanut butter, at room temperature.

CHOCOLATE CHEESECAKE ICING

Add an additional ½ cup confectioners' sugar and ½ cup unsweetened cocoa powder.

PEANUT BUTTER CINNAMON CHEESECAKE ICING

Add ½ cup smooth peanut butter, at room temperature, and 1 tablespoon ground cinnamon.

CUPCAKE ASSORTMENT

Cupcakes are incredibly versatile: you can make them big or small; you can stuff them, you can ice them—it just depends on whatever you or the people you love like to eat.

CEREAL ICING

This icing adds a touch of fun to any cake. Be sure to use a colorful—and sugared—cereal. Pulse the cereal in a food processor or crush it in a plastic bag with a rolling pin until it is the texture of sand with pebbles in it.

½ pound (2 sticks) unsalted butter, at room temperature

1 teaspoon pure vanilla extract

3 cups confectioners' sugar

½ teaspoon fine sea salt

½ cup finely ground Fruity Pebbles

↳ *I also like to use Froot Loops, Golden Grahams, and Frosted Flakes*

1. With a hand mixer or a stand mixer fitted with the whisk attachment, whip the butter on high speed for 1 minute. Add the vanilla and whip just to incorporate.

2. With the mixer on low speed, gradually add the confectioners' sugar, 1 cup at a time, and mix until completely incorporated, scraping down the sides of the bowl between additions. Add the salt and whip on high speed for 3 minutes more.

3. With a spatula, fold in the ground cereal and mix just until combined.

PRETZEL ICING

I love salty and sweet and I love doing things differently. Pretzels work really well in the icing because the icing texture comes through first and then you get the salty taste at the end. I like to use gluten-free pretzels—they're the crunchiest. Crush them very fine using either a food processor or a rolling pan (place the pretzels in a plastic bag first). You want them to be fine enough to fit through the tip of the piping bag.

½ pound (2 sticks) unsalted butter, at room temperature

1 teaspoon pure vanilla extract

3 cups confectioners' sugar

½ teaspoon fine sea salt

½ cup finely ground gluten-free pretzels

They're crunchier!

1. With a hand mixer or a stand mixer fitted with the whisk attachment, whip the butter on high speed for 1 minute. Add the vanilla and whip just to incorporate.

2. With the mixer on low speed, gradually add the confectioners' sugar, 1 cup at a time, and mix until completely incorporated, scraping down the sides of the bowl between additions. Add the salt and whip on high speed for 3 minutes more.

3. With a spatula, fold in the ground pretzels and mix just until combined.

CHOCOLATE PRETZEL ICING

Add 1 cup unsweetened cocoa powder with the confectioners' sugar.

REAL MINT ICING (NANA ICING)

I don't use a lot of food coloring, but taste is dependent on the visual, so I want you to see that this icing is green and it's mint. I'm leaving the amount of food coloring up to you. I used a drop to enhance the color, but you could use more if you'd like to make it brighter.

½ cup granulated sugar

⅓ cup packed fresh mint leaves

½ pound (2 sticks) unsalted butter, at room temperature

1 teaspoon pure vanilla extract

2 teaspoons freshly squeezed lemon juice

3½ cups confectioners' sugar

¼ teaspoon fine sea salt

1 drop each of green and yellow food coloring (optional)

1. With a hand mixer or a food processor, combine the granulated sugar and mint leaves and process until the leaves are completely incorporated and the same consistency as the sugar.

2. In the bowl of a stand mixer fitted with the whisk attachment, whip the butter on high speed for 1 minute. Add the mint sugar and whip until fluffy. Scrape down the sides of the bowl and add the vanilla and lemon juice and whip just to incorporate.

3. With the mixer on low speed, gradually add the confectioners' sugar, 1 cup at a time, then the salt, mixing until completely incorporated, scraping down the sides of the bowl between additions. Add the food coloring, if using, and whip on high speed for 3 minutes more.

CAKE BATTER ICING

Once I succeeded in making cookie dough icings, you'd have to guess that cake batter wouldn't be far behind. Don't make the actual cake batter—you're just using the mix as an ingredient.

You don't need vanilla extract because it's already in the mix!

½ pound (2 sticks) unsalted butter, at room temperature

1 box store-bought yellow cake mix

½ teaspoon fine sea salt

½ cup heavy cream, at room temperature

1. With a hand mixer or a stand mixer fitted with the whisk attachment, whip the butter on high speed for 1 minute.

2. With the mixer on low speed, gradually add the cake mix and salt and mix until completely incorporated. Scrape down the sides of the bowl, then whip on high speed for 3 minutes more.

3. Add the cream and whip on high speed until incorporated, about 2 minutes.

PUMPKIN SPICE LATTE ICING

½ pound (2 sticks) unsalted butter, at room temperature

¼ cup brewed espresso, cooled

1 teaspoon pure vanilla extract

3¾ cups confectioners' sugar

1 tablespoon pumpkin pie spice (see page 127)

¼ teaspoon fine sea salt

Orange food coloring (optional)

1. With a hand mixer or a stand mixer fitted with the whisk attachment, whip the butter on high speed for 1 minute. Add the espresso and vanilla and whip just to incorporate.

2. With the mixer on low speed, gradually add the sugar, pumpkin pie spice, and salt and mix until completely incorporated, scraping down the sides of the bowl between additions. Add the food coloring, if using, and whip on high speed for 3 minutes more.

PUMPKIN SPICE ICING

½ pound (2 sticks) unsalted butter, at room temperature

1 teaspoon pure vanilla extract

3¾ cups confectioners' sugar

1 tablespoon pumpkin pie spice (see page 127)

¼ teaspoon fine sea salt

1. With a hand mixer or a stand mixer fitted with the whisk attachment, whip the butter on high speed for 1 minute. Add the vanilla and whip just to incorporate.

2. With the mixer on low speed, gradually add the sugar, pumpkin pie spice, and salt and mix until completely incorporated, scraping down the sides of the bowl between additions. Whip on high speed for 3 minutes more.

BROWNIE BATTER ICING

I use Betty Crocker Fudge Brownie mix, but feel free to use the same amount of your favorite brand. Don't make the brownie batter; you're just using the mix as an ingredient.

½ pound (2 sticks) unsalted butter, at room temperature

One 18.3-ounce box store-bought brownie mix

¼ teaspoon fine sea salt

½ cup heavy cream, at room temperature

1. With a hand mixer or a stand mixer fitted with the whisk attachment, whip the butter on high speed for 1 minute.

2. With the mixer on low speed, gradually add the brownie mix and salt and mix until completely incorporated. Scrape down the sides of the bowl, then whip on high speed for 3 minutes more.

3. Add the cream and whip on high speed until incorporated, about 30 seconds.

COCONUT ICING

Top Coconut Cake (page 148) with this icing and you'll have an explosion of natural coconut flavor.

8 tablespoons (1 stick) unsalted butter, at room temperature

One 13.5-ounce can full-fat coconut milk, solids only (do not shake the can before opening; pour off the liquid for another use)

1 teaspoon pure vanilla extract

½ teaspoon coconut extract

3¾ cups confectioners' sugar

½ teaspoon fine sea salt

1. With a hand mixer or a stand mixer fitted with the whisk attachment, whip the butter and the coconut solids on high speed for 1 minute. Add the vanilla and coconut extract and whip just to incorporate.

2. With the mixer on low speed, gradually add the sugar and salt and mix until completely incorporated. Scrape down the sides of the bowl, then whip on high speed for 3 minutes more.

WHIPPED VANILLA ICING

Some people don't like all the sweetness and sugar of regular icing. So instead, you could take almost any flavor profile in the icings section and make it with whipped cream. I love to use whipped cream as a filling; it's light and cold and delicious.

2 cups heavy cream, at room temperature

1 teaspoon pure vanilla extract

½ cup confectioners' sugar

1. If possible, chill the bowl and the whisk attachment of a hand or stand mixer for at least half an hour before using. All of your ingredients should be cold.

2. Pour the cream, vanilla, and sugar into the chilled bowl and whip on high speed until stiff peaks form, about 2 minutes.

WHIPPED CHOCOLATE ICING
. . . .

Add ¼ cup unsweetened cocoa powder with the cream, vanilla, and sugar.

WHIPPED NUTELLA ICING
. . . .

Add ½ cup room-temperature Nutella with the cream, vanilla, and sugar.

WHIPPED PEANUT BUTTER ICING

Add ½ cup room-temperature smooth peanut butter with the cream, vanilla, and sugar.

WHIPPED CHOCOLATE PEANUT BUTTER ICING

Add ½ cup room-temperature smooth peanut butter and ¼ cup unsweetened cocoa powder with the cream, vanilla, and sugar.

WHIPPED CINNAMON ICING

Add 1 teaspoon ground cinnamon with the cream, vanilla, and sugar.

WHIPPED ESPRESSO ICING

Add ¼ cup brewed espresso, chilled, with the cream, vanilla, and sugar.

WHIPPED DOUGHNUT ICING

Add ½ teaspoon mace with the cream, vanilla, and sugar.

WHIPPED PUMPKIN SPICE ICING

Add 1 teaspoon pumpkin pie spice (see page 127) with the cream, vanilla, and sugar.

WHIPPED PUMPKIN SPICE LATTE ICING

Add ¼ cup brewed espresso, chilled, and 2 teaspoons pumpkin pie spice (see page 127) with the cream, vanilla, and sugar.

WHIPPED MAPLE ICING

Add ½ teaspoon maple extract with the cream, vanilla, and sugar.

WHIPPED MATCHA ICING

Add 1 tablespoon plus 1 teaspoon matcha green tea powder with the cream, vanilla, and sugar.

WHIPPED LEMON ICING

Add 1 teaspoon grated lemon zest and 1 teaspoon freshly squeezed lemon juice with the cream, vanilla, and sugar.

WHIPPED DULCE DE LECHE ICING

Omit the confectioners' sugar and add 1 cup store-bought dulce de leche, at room temperature, with the cream and vanilla.

WHIPPED SALTED CARAMEL ICING

Omit the confectioners' sugar and add 1 cup store-bought dulce de leche, at room temperature, and 1 teaspoon fine sea salt with the cream and vanilla.

WHIPPED HOT COCOA ICING

Omit the confectioners' sugar and add ¾ cup store-bought hot cocoa mix (I like Swiss Miss) with the cream and vanilla.

CHOCOLATE SUNDAE CUPCAKES

CAKE: Grandma Annie's Chocolate Cake (page 89)

ICING: Whipped Vanilla Icing (page 204)

FILLING: Store-bought chocolate fudge sauce

TOPPINGS: Store-bought hot fudge, rainbow sprinkles, nonpareils, and cherries

This was the very first Mini of the Month we ever served at Baked by Melissa. At the time, having to come up with a new flavor every month scared the shit out of me, which is ironic because now we produce twenty-four new flavors every year, not including the promotional flavors that we do for holidays. And I create every one. It just goes to show what can happen when you push yourself out of your comfort zone.

We started the Mini of the Month concept in 2009 and now each of our bakeries does it. It's a way to bring customers back and keep things exciting. For me, the variations are a way to keep me challenged. I love the idea of creating something new and different all the time. As you get older, it's important to keep using your brain (use it or lose it) and the same is true of creativity (you don't want to get stale). I love the challenge to be constantly creating, and I think it makes me better at what I do.

For this cupcake, I thought about what I love about ice cream. It replicates a traditional ice cream sundae: chocolate cake stuffed with store-bought chocolate fudge sauce and iced with a whipped cream icing. You also could use regular vanilla icing. I like to use a special star tip on the piping bag that makes the cream look like it came right out of the Reddi-wip can. Top each cupcake with a mix of rainbow sprinkles and nonpareils and a drizzle of hot fudge. And of course there's a cherry on top.

BERRY CAKE

....

CAKE: **Classic Vanilla Cake**

FILLINGS: **Whipped Vanilla Icing and mixed fresh berries**

ICING: **Whipped Vanilla Icing**

TOPPINGS: **Mixed fresh berries, fresh mint sprigs, and confectioners' sugar**

....

This cake is fancy. It's for when you want a pretty cake that's also light and delicious.

One of the many reasons I like to cut round cakes from a sheet pan (see page 20 for the other benefits) is that it automatically gives you layers with a neat, trimmed edge with no brown crust. You can leave the sides exposed, which is a very pretty effect and shows off your fillings.

1 recipe Classic Vanilla Cake (page 34)

1 recipe Whipped Vanilla Icing (page 204)

2 to 3 cups mixed fresh berries (whatever's in season)

Fresh mint sprigs, for garnish

Confectioners' sugar, for dusting

1. Preheat the oven to 350°F. Butter a 13 x 18-inch half-sheet pan, then line it with wax paper or parchment and butter the paper.

2. Mix the cake batter according to the recipe directions. Pour into the prepared pan and bake until the middle of the cake feels springy when you gently press your finger against it (see page 30), 35 to 40 minutes.

3. Set aside to cool completely. Meanwhile, make the whipped vanilla icing and stash it in the freezer until you're ready to frost the cake.

4. Use a 6-inch round cutter to cut three rounds from the cake. Place one cake layer on a turntable and thickly frost the top with about a third of the vanilla icing; spread the icing out just over the edge of the layer. Spoon a few tablespoons of fruit on top. Repeat with the remaining layers, until reaching the final layer.

5. Generously top the cake with the remaining mixed berries. Garnish with the sprigs of mint and lightly dust with confectioners' sugar.

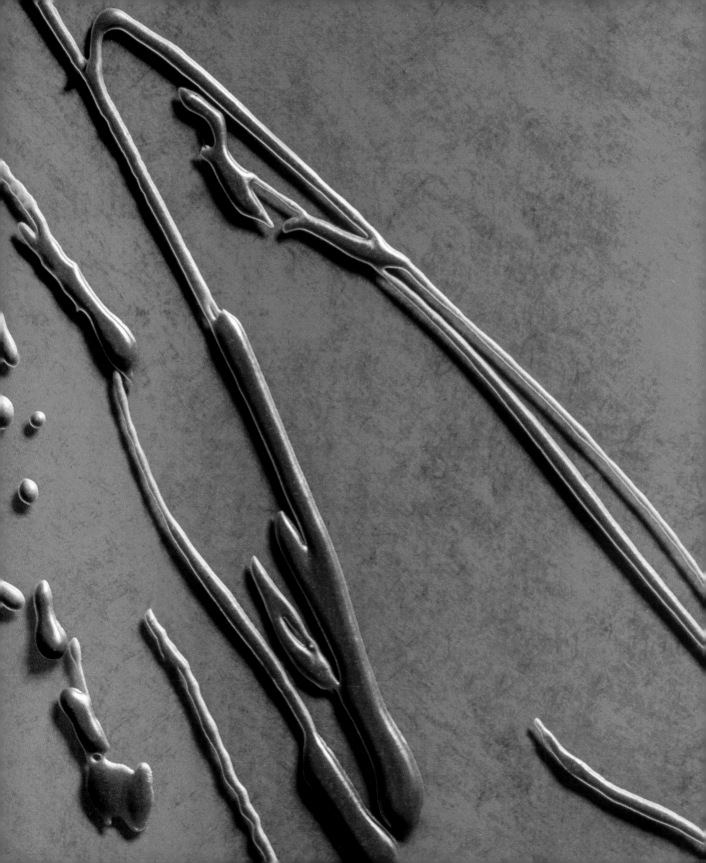

GLAZES

A glaze is the perfect garnish. It adds flavor and is great for hiding your mistakes or making the cake look pretty. Glazes are great on Bundt cakes, and when you crumb coat a layer cake with buttercream icing. You can add a glaze to drip down the sides. Glazes are very simple to make—most are just confectioners' sugar with a little bit of liquid, usually whole milk—and you can dye a glaze any color.

Start by making your glaze thicker than you want. You can always add more milk, but you can't take it away. Remember that humidity will change the consistency of a glaze, as will the addition of food coloring.

Consider the milk measurement in the glaze recipes as approximate, because the amount you add depends on the consistency you want—do you want the drips to go down all the way? Halfway down? Or just stay on top? If you want the glaze to be like a shellac, a very thick mixture will give you a glistening coat.

To decide whether a glaze has the right consistency, dip a spoon in it and then lift it up—when you get a smooth ribbon drip, the glaze is ready. It's all about what that drip looks like when you hold the spoon up in the air, because that's what's going to happen on the cake. Your glaze is not done until you can see a single ribbon dripping from the spoon back into the bowl. When you first see the ribbon, it will be more of a blob, and you can stop there. If you want more of a drip, add more milk.

If you're not using the glaze within 10 minutes of mixing, cover the bowl with plastic wrap to keep the glaze from drying out. Store at room temperature.

GLAZE YIELDS

Each glaze recipe makes about ⅔ cup—enough to glaze one 9-inch cake, 12 regular-size doughnuts, one 6-cup Bundt, or 24 mini cupcakes.

VANILLA GLAZE

2 cups confectioners'
sugar

4 tablespoons
whole milk, at room
temperature, plus more
as needed

½ teaspoon pure vanilla
extract

You can also mix the glaze by hand using a whisk or a spoon.

1. With a hand mixer or a stand mixer fitted with the whisk attachment, combine the confectioners' sugar, milk, and vanilla. Mix on low speed until smooth. If the glaze is too thick, add a little more milk to thin it to the desired consistency.

2. If not using within 10 minutes of mixing, cover the bowl with plastic wrap to keep the glaze from drying out. Store at room temperature.

CAKE DOUGHNUTS

. . . .

CAKES: **Doughnut Cake (page 66) and Grandma Annie's Chocolate Cake (page 89)**

GLAZES: **Chocolate Glaze (page 222) and Vanilla Glaze (page 218)**

TOPPINGS: **Sprinkles, nonpareils, sanding sugar, Fruity Pebbles, coarse sea salt, crushed Oreo cookies**

. . . .

Doughnuts are delicious, and these are baked, not fried. I bake any cake recipe in a doughnut pan (I have two: a mini and a regular size) and then have fun decorating them. These are vanilla and chocolate cake doughnuts covered with chocolate and vanilla glazes in many-colored variations. To get the marbleized effect, dip the doughnut all the way to the bottom of all the different colored glazes. Sprinkle on the toppings, right away before the glaze starts to harden. It's a superfun activity and I really suggest doing this with your kids—it's just like decorating sugar cookies.

CHOCOLATE GLAZE

2 cups confectioners' sugar

½ cup unsweetened cocoa powder

½ cup plus 1 tablespoon whole milk, at room temperature, plus more as needed

½ teaspoon pure vanilla extract

2 pinches of fine sea salt

1. Sift the sugar into a large mixing bowl. Add the cocoa powder, milk, vanilla, and salt and whisk or stir with a spoon until smooth. If the glaze is too thick, add a little more milk to thin it to the desired consistency.

2. If not using within 10 minutes of mixing, cover the bowl with plastic wrap to keep the glaze from drying out. Store at room temperature.

SAMOA DOUGHNUTS

....

CAKE: **Classic Vanilla Cake**

GLAZE: **Chocolate Glaze**

TOPPINGS: **Store-bought caramel sauce, unsweetened shredded coconut**

....

With a doughnut pan, you can turn any cake batter into a doughnut that's baked rather than fried. These are a fun take on one of my favorite Girl Scout cookies: Samoas. Once the doughnuts are baked, let them cool, then place on a rack and spoon chocolate glaze on top. Let the glaze do its thing. Top with shredded and toasted coconut mixed with store-bought caramel topping, and then more chocolate glaze.

1 recipe Classic Vanilla Cake (page 34)

1⅓ cups unsweetened shredded coconut

2 recipes Chocolate Glaze (page 222)

1 cup store-bought caramel sauce

¼ teaspoon coarse sea salt

1. Preheat the oven to 350°F. Butter a 12-count doughnut pan.

2. Mix the vanilla cake batter according to the recipe directions. Divide among the doughnut cups and bake until the middle of a cupcake feels springy when you gently press your finger against it (see page 30), 20 to 25 minutes.

3. Transfer the doughnuts to a rack to cool—just dump them out of the pan or remove them as soon as they're cool enough to handle. (They'll cool faster out of the pan and I'm impatient!)

4. Spread ⅔ cup of the shredded coconut on a parchment-lined quarter-sheet pan and toast in the oven, stirring occasionally, until lightly browned, about 10 minutes. Set the toasted coconut aside to cool, then mix with the remaining coconut.

5. Meanwhile, make a double recipe of the chocolate glaze according to the recipe directions.

6. Place some parchment paper under the rack (to catch all the drips) and spoon the glaze over the doughnuts to completely coat the tops. Mix the coconut with the caramel sauce and, applying by hand, cover the tops.

7. Fill a disposable pastry bag with the remaining chocolate glaze. Snip the tip and drizzle the tops of the doughnuts with stripes of chocolate.

STRAWBERRY GLAZE

2 cups confectioners' sugar

¼ cup strawberry puree (page 53)

2 teaspoons whole milk, at room temperature, plus more as needed

1 teaspoon freshly squeezed lemon juice

½ teaspoon pure vanilla extract

1. Sift the sugar into a mixing bowl. Add the strawberry puree, milk, lemon juice, and vanilla and whisk or stir with a spoon until smooth.

2. If the glaze is too thick, add a little more milk to thin it to the desired consistency.

3. If not using within 10 minutes of mixing, cover the bowl with plastic wrap to keep the glaze from drying out. Store it at room temperature.

LEMON GLAZE

2 cups confectioners' sugar

½ teaspoon grated lemon zest

2 tablespoons freshly squeezed lemon juice

2 teaspoons whole milk, at room temperature, plus more as needed

½ teaspoon pure vanilla extract

1. With a hand mixer or a stand mixer fitted with the whisk attachment, combine the confectioners' sugar, lemon zest and juice, milk, and vanilla extract. Mix on low speed until smooth. If the glaze is too thick, add a little more milk to thin it to the desired consistency.

2. If not using within 10 minutes of mixing, cover the bowl with plastic wrap to keep the glaze from drying out. Store it at room temperature.

CINNAMON GLAZE

2 cups confectioners' sugar

¼ cup whole milk, at room temperature, plus more as needed

1 teaspoon ground cinnamon

½ teaspoon pure vanilla extract

1. With a hand mixer or a stand mixer fitted with the whisk attachment, combine the confectioners' sugar, milk, cinnamon, and vanilla extract. Mix on low speed until smooth. If the glaze is too thick, add a little more milk to thin it to the desired consistency.

2. If not using within 10 minutes of mixing, cover the bowl with plastic wrap to keep the glaze from drying out. Store it at room temperature.

ESPRESSO GLAZE

2 cups confectioners' sugar

¼ cup brewed espresso, at room temperature

½ teaspoon pure vanilla extract

Whole milk, at room temperature, as needed

1. Sift the sugar into a mixing bowl. Add the espresso and vanilla and whisk or stir with a spoon until smooth. If the glaze is too thick, add a little whole milk to thin it to the desired consistency.

2. If not using within 10 minutes of mixing, cover the bowl with plastic wrap to keep the glaze from drying out. Store it at room temperature.

PUMPKIN SPICE GLAZE

2 cups confectioners' sugar

¼ cup whole milk, plus more as needed

½ teaspoon pure vanilla extract

½ teaspoon pumpkin pie spice (see page 127)

2 drops orange food coloring (optional)

1. With a hand mixer or a stand mixer fitted with the whisk attachment, combine the confectioners' sugar, milk, vanilla, pumpkin pie spice, and food coloring, if using. Mix on low speed until smooth. If the glaze is too thick, add a little more milk to thin it to the desired consistency.

2. If not using within 10 minutes of mixing, cover the bowl with plastic wrap to keep the glaze from drying out. Store it at room temperature.

HOT COCOA GLAZE

The amount of milk needed may vary depending on the brand of cocoa. Use your eye and the photo on page 233 as a reference.

2 cups store-bought hot cocoa mix

¼ cup plus 2 teaspoons whole milk, at room temperature, plus more as needed

½ teaspoon pure vanilla extract

1. With a hand mixer or a stand mixer fitted with the whisk attachment, combine the hot cocoa mix, milk, and vanilla extract. Mix on low speed until smooth. If the glaze is too thick, add a little more milk to thin it to the desired consistency.

2. If not using within 10 minutes of mixing, cover the bowl with plastic wrap to keep the glaze from drying out. Store it at room temperature.

MARSHMALLOW FLUFF GLAZE

2 cups Marshmallow Fluff

2 tablespoons whole milk, at room temperature, plus more as needed

½ teaspoon pure vanilla extract

1. With a hand mixer or a stand mixer fitted with the whisk attachment, combine the Marshmallow Fluff, milk, and vanilla extract. Mix on low speed until smooth. If the glaze is too thick, add a little more milk to thin it to the desired consistency.

2. If not using within 10 minutes of mixing, cover the bowl with plastic wrap to keep the glaze from drying out. Store it at room temperature.

MATCHA GLAZE

2 cups confectioners' sugar

¼ cup whole milk, at room temperature, plus more as needed

2 teaspoons matcha green tea powder

1 teaspoon freshly squeezed lemon juice

½ teaspoon pure vanilla extract

1. With a hand mixer or a stand mixer fitted with the whisk attachment, combine the confectioners' sugar, milk, matcha powder, lemon juice, and vanilla extract. Mix on low speed until smooth. If the glaze is too thick, add a little more milk to thin it to the desired consistency.

2. If not using within 10 minutes of mixing, cover the bowl with plastic wrap to keep the glaze from drying out. Store it at room temperature.

MAPLE GLAZE

2 cups confectioners' sugar

½ cup Grade A very dark maple syrup

¼ cup whole milk, at room temperature, plus more as needed

½ teaspoon pure vanilla extract

1. With a hand mixer or a stand mixer fitted with the whisk attachment, combine the confectioners' sugar, maple syrup, milk, and vanilla extract. Mix on low speed until smooth. If the glaze is too thick, add a little more milk to thin it to the desired consistency.

2. If not using within 10 minutes of mixing, cover the bowl with plastic wrap to keep the glaze from drying out. Store it at room temperature.

CARAMEL GLAZE

2 cups granulated sugar

1 cup heavy cream, at room temperature

8 tablespoons (1 stick) unsalted butter

1 teaspoon baking soda

1 teaspoon fine sea salt

1. In a heavy-bottomed pan set over medium heat, combine the sugar, cream, butter, baking soda, and salt. Cook, stirring constantly, until the sugar has melted and big bubbles start to form on the surface. Remove immediately from the heat and, stirring constantly, let cool for 3 to 5 minutes.

2. Immediately spoon the glaze over your cake and let it cool. If the glaze thickens too much before you use it, place it back on the heat until it returns to a liquid.

SALTED CARAMEL GLAZE

2 cups granulated sugar

1 cup heavy cream, at room temperature

8 tablespoons (1 stick) unsalted butter

1 teaspoon baking soda

3 teaspoons fine sea salt

1. In a heavy-bottomed pan set over medium heat, combine the sugar, cream, butter, baking soda, and salt. Cook, stirring constantly, until the sugar has melted and big bubbles start to form on the surface. Remove immediately from the heat and, stirring constantly, let cool for 3 to 5 minutes.

2. Immediately spoon the glaze over your cake and let it cool. If the glaze thickens too much before you use it, place it back on the heat until it returns to a liquid.

PEANUT BUTTER GLAZE I

2 to 4 cups smooth peanut butter, preferably natural

Place the peanut butter in a microwave-safe bowl and zap on high until the peanut butter has melted to a liquid consistency, about 1 minute, depending on your microwave. You can also melt the peanut butter in a heavy-bottomed pan set over medium heat. Stir constantly while cooking. See this glaze in real life on page 90.

PEANUT BUTTER GLAZE II

1 cup smooth peanut butter, preferably natural, at room temperature

2 cups confectioners' sugar

¾ cup plus 2 tablespoons whole milk, at room temperature

With a hand mixer or a stand mixer fitted with the whisk attachment, whip the peanut butter on high speed for 1 minute. Reduce the mixer speed to low and gradually add the confectioners' sugar, 1 cup at a time, then the milk, mixing until thoroughly incorporated. Increase the speed and whip to fully combine.

TOPPINGS

A cake or cupcake is never finished without that little extra something on top. Crumbles and other toppings add one last layer of flavor and a nice texture. They're a great finishing touch. In fact, some of my favorite cakes aren't iced at all; they're topped with crumbles or crumbs. We launched muffins at Baked by Melissa in December 2016 and use crumble toppings for a lot of them.

I'm influenced by those classic Entenmann's crumb cakes and my dad's babka. He doesn't like overly sweet things, so I use a thin layer of icing and a chocolate crumble as a garnish. I pile the top high with crumbs, which add both flavor and texture. They're also a great snack while or after baking.

A crumble can transform a cake into a completely different flavor profile. Topping Grandma Sylvia's Blueberry Cake (page 58) with Graham Cracker Crumble (page 242) or Cinnamon Crumble (page 242) makes it more like a breakfast pastry. You also could make the Blueberry Cake with the Cinnamon Crumble into a delicious muffin. YUM.

That classic crumble-topped coffee cake from your local deli or bakery that comes in chocolate or vanilla? You can make it in any flavor you like! You can also add a crumble to any cake batter before it goes in the oven.

Chocolate Crumble (page 243) is my new obsession—and it's even better when left unbaked. I like it better than cookie dough (gasp!).

Most of all, toppings are fun. Who wouldn't smile when presented with a cake ringed with cookie dough and Oreo cookies? These are the ultimate mix-and-match components.

CRUMBLES

Here's a perfect example of how you can mix and match the cakes and the crumbles—each will give you a unique flavor experience that's based on what you or someone you love wants to eat.

A few pairing suggestions, from top to bottom: Cinnamon Cake (page 60) with cinnamon crumble, Classic Vanilla Cake (page 34) with Funfetti crumble (my personal favorite), Grandma Annie's Chocolate Cake (page 89) with cinnamon crumble, Classic Vanilla Cake with shortbread crumble (which tastes like heaven on earth), Grandma Sylvia's Blueberry Cake (page 58) with graham cracker crumble, Grandma Annie's Chocolate Cake with chocolate crumble, and Cereal Cake (page 79) with cereal crumble.

I suggest using a springform pan for any cake that you'll be topping with a crumble, as they'll stay perfect and won't break up when you remove the cake from the pan.

1. With a hand mixer or a stand mixer fitted with the paddle attachment, combine the dry ingredients. Mix on low speed while gradually pouring in the melted butter.

2. Continue to mix until a crumbly consistency is achieved, about 30 seconds. Store in an airtight container in the fridge for up to a week. Use to top any cake or cupcake either before or after baking and icing.

CINNAMON CRUMBLE

1 cup all-purpose flour

⅔ cup sugar

1 teaspoon ground cinnamon

¼ teaspoon fine sea salt

8 tablespoons (1 stick) unsalted butter, melted

GRAHAM CRACKER CRUMBLE

1 cup ground graham crackers

¼ teaspoon fine sea salt

6 tablespoons unsalted butter, melted

OREO CRUMBLE

1 cup crushed Oreo cookies

¼ teaspoon fine sea salt

4 tablespoons (½ stick) unsalted butter, melted

CEREAL CRUMBLE

1 cup all-purpose flour

⅔ cup sugar

⅓ cup ground Fruity Pebbles cereal

¼ teaspoon fine sea salt

8 tablespoons (1 stick) unsalted butter, melted

The cereal should be ground to a sandy consistency.

My favorite!

CHOCOLATE CRUMBLE

1 cup all-purpose flour

⅔ cup sugar

¼ cup unsweetened cocoa powder

¼ teaspoon fine sea salt

10 tablespoons unsalted butter, melted

FUNFETTI CRUMBLE

1 cup all-purpose flour

⅔ cup sugar

¼ teaspoon fine sea salt

8 tablespoons (1 stick) unsalted butter, melted

⅓ cup rainbow sprinkles

Mix in the sprinkles at the end.

SHORTBREAD CRUMBLE

1 cup all-purpose flour

⅔ cup sugar

¼ teaspoon fine sea salt

8 tablespoons (1 stick) unsalted butter, melted

CHOCOLATE CHIP COOKIE DOUGH TOPPING

½ pound (2 sticks) unsalted butter, at room temperature

2 teaspoons pure vanilla extract

1½ cups all-purpose flour

1½ cups packed light brown sugar

1 teaspoon fine sea salt

½ cup micro chocolate chips (see page 24)

With a hand mixer or a stand mixer fitted with the whisk attachment, whip the butter on high speed for 2 minutes. Add the vanilla and whip just to incorporate. With the mixer on low speed, gradually add the flour, brown sugar, and salt and mix until incorporated, scraping down the sides of the bowl between additions. Increase the speed to high and whip for 1 minute. With a spatula, fold in the chocolate chips.

SUGAR COOKIE DOUGH TOPPING

½ pound (2 sticks) unsalted butter, at room temperature

2 teaspoons pure vanilla extract

1⅓ cups sugar

1¼ cups all-purpose flour

1 teaspoon fine sea salt

With a hand mixer or a stand mixer fitted with the whisk attachment, whip the butter on high speed for 1 minute. Add the vanilla and whip just to incorporate. Add the sugar and whip for 1 minute. Scrape down the sides of the bowl. Add the flour and salt and whip just until incorporated. Scrape down the sides of the bowl one last time.

COCONUT FILLING/ TOPPING

½ cup unsweetened shredded coconut

½ cup deciccated coconut

½ cup sweetened condensed milk

¼ teaspoon fine sea salt

With a hand mixer or a stand mixer, combine the shredded and desiccated coconut, condensed milk, and salt. Pulse until fully combined.

COCONUT GOO

2 cups unsweetened shredded coconut

About ½ cup sweetened condensed milk

Pinch of fine sea salt

1. Place the coconut in the work bowl of a food processor. Adjust the amount of milk to get the texture you're looking for: if you want a topping, use less (it should be the consistency of cookie dough); if you want a filling, use a little more milk (so that it can be used in a piping bag).

2. Add the milk 1 tablespoon at a time, pulsing until you get a smooth consistency. Add the salt and pulse just to combine.

It's the middle of an Almond Joy—freakin' delicious!

CHOCOLATE CHIP COOKIE DOUGH CUPCAKES

CAKE: **Classic Vanilla Cake**

FILLING: **Chocolate Chip Cookie Dough Icing**

ICING: **Chocolate Icing**

TOPPINGS: **Chocolate Chip Cookie Dough Topping and nonpareils**

This is one of the original Baked by Melissa cupcake combinations and still one of my favorites—a vanilla cupcake filled with chocolate chip cookie dough icing and topped with chocolate icing and more chocolate chip cookie dough icing.

Unsalted butter, for greasing the pan

1 recipe Classic Vanilla Cake (page 34)

1 recipe Chocolate Chip Cookie Dough Icing (page 178)

1 recipe Chocolate Icing (page 168)

½ cup rainbow nonpareils

1. Preheat the oven to 350°F. Butter the wells of a 24-count mini cupcake pan, or line the wells with mini paper baking liners.

2. Mix and bake the cake batter according to the recipe directions. Set the cupcakes aside to cool completely.

3. Meanwhile, make the chocolate chip cookie dough icing and chocolate icing according to the recipe directions.

4. Fill a disposable pastry bag with half the chocolate chip cookie dough icing and snip the tip of the bag about ½ inch from the end. Puncture a hole in the top of a cupcake with the tip of the pastry bag and slowly squeeze the bag to fill the cupcake. The cupcake will plump a bit, but do not fill it so much that it breaks. Repeat with the remaining cupcakes.

5. Fit another disposable pastry bag with a round tip. Fill the bag with chocolate icing and pipe a swirl on top of each cupcake.

6. Top the cupcakes with chunks of the cookie dough topping and decorate with nonpareils.

SLUTTY CAKE

CAKE: Classic Vanilla Cake, brownies, chocolate chip cookie dough

FILLING: Cookies and Cream Icing

ICING: Chocolate Icing

GLAZE: Vanilla Glaze *For this cake, I dyed it pink!*

TOPPINGS: Chocolate Chip Cookie Dough Topping, baked brownies, Oreo cookie chunks, sprinkles, and nonpareils

I love slutty brownies. They usually consist of a cookie dough layer, plus brownies, plus Oreos, plus whatever else you like. This is my version as a cake.

I don't usually plan the decorations too much in advance—I like to wing it. I love chocolate icing with vanilla cake, so I knew there would be chocolate icing, but I like the cake to look colorful and pretty, so that's where the pink glaze comes in. That's vanilla glaze with a couple of dots of electric pink food coloring. When it comes to food coloring, just do what feels good to you—continue adding drops until you get a color you like. Same with the glaze consistency: add a little more milk until it comes to the consistency that you like. You want it nice and drippy.

The cake is topped with chunks of cookie dough, brownie, and Oreo cookies. I love to top my cakes and cupcakes with whatever flavor is inside. If I'm going to eat something, I want to know what it's going to taste like just by looking at it.

As for the sprinkles . . . I put sprinkles on everything.

Unsalted butter, for greasing the pan

1 recipe Classic Vanilla Cake (page 34)

Two 18.3-ounce boxes store-bought brownie mix (plus required ingredients)

Two 16.5-ounce packages store-bought chocolate chip cookie dough

1 recipe Cookies and Cream Icing (page 176)

1 recipe Chocolate Icing (page 168)

1 recipe Vanilla Glaze (page 218)

Electric pink food coloring

Chocolate Chip Cookie Dough Topping (page 244)

Baked brownie pieces, for topping

1 sleeve Oreo cookies, broken in half, for topping

½ cup rainbow sprinkles and nonpareils, mixed

Who better to share a Slutty Cake or two with than your oldest and dearest friends? Bari (far left) was maid of honor at my wedding—we met in summer camp and became best friends at nine years old; Laura (standing) grew up down the street from me. She's my only close friend with kids, so whenever I have a question about Scottie, I call her. Seated next to Laura is Julie. We met in middle school and have remained close friends ever since. Next to me (hi!) is another Melissa, but we call her Mel. She's taught me so much in life. She's always so happy and genuinely interested in you. Next to Mel is Jen, who also grew up down the street from me. Our group of friends would go to her house after school and make all those crazy food concoctions. Jen's sister Carly famously stayed with me during her summer internship at Alison Brod Public Relations. She brought my cupcakes to work and the rest is history.

1. Preheat the oven to 350°F. Butter a 13 x 18-inch half-sheet pan, or line it with wax paper or parchment and butter the paper. Butter or line two 13 x 9-inch pans for one box of brownies.

2. Mix the vanilla cake batter according to the recipe directions. Mix one box of the brownie batter according to the instructions on the box. Spread the brownie batter over the half-sheet pan. Pour half of the cake batter directly on top and spread it evenly over the brownie layer.

3. Press one package of the cookie dough into one 13 x 9-inch prepared pan. Pour the remaining vanilla cake batter directly on top.

4. Mix the second box of brownie batter according to the directions. Pour the batter into the other 13 x 9-inch pan.

5. Bake the slutty cakes until the middle of the cake feels springy when you gently press your finger against it (see page 30), about 40 minutes. Bake the brownies according to the package directions.

6. Set the cakes and the brownies aside to cool completely. Once cooled, cut the cake into 8½-inch rounds

7. Meanwhile, make the cookies and cream and chocolate icings according to the recipe directions. Frost the top of the cookie-cake layer with cookies and cream icing. Set the brownie-cake layer on top, then frost the entire cake with the chocolate icing.

8. Make the vanilla glaze right before you're ready to finish the cake. Pour the glaze over the top of the cake and let it drip down the sides. Top with a ring of alternating chunks of the cookie dough topping, baked brownies pieces, and Oreo cookies and decorate with the sprinkle mix.

DARK CHOCOLATE MUNCHIE BRITTLE AND DARK CHOCOLATE RAINBOW BRITTLE

I use brittles as garnishes on our cupcakes. It's a way for me to include color and tie everything together visually, but also to add texture, so you get a little crunch with your cake. Brittles also make great snacks. I grew up eating those huge dark chocolate bars from Trader Joe's. My mother always kept them in the pantry and I'd break off a square every night before I went to bed. That's what brittle is for me—a quick sweet bite to satisfy a craving. And it lasts for a while, so you can store it in a jar or a plastic bag.

There are two methods for making chocolate brittle—for one, you melt chocolate and add mix-ins; with the other you drizzle melted chocolate over the sprinkles (or other crunchy bits). The Dark Chocolate Munchie Brittle is melted chocolate with Cape Cod potato chips and gluten-free pretzels thrown in. I spread the mixture out on wax paper while the chocolate is still warm. That brittle is my kind of snack. (And yes, you should use Cape Cod potato chips and gluten-free pretzels because they're both the crunchiest kinds you can find.) Then I hit it with a little sprinkle of sea salt.

I make the rainbow brittle differently, so the color of the garnish can be seen. I spread the sprinkles in a sheet pan and drizzle melted chocolate on top. The result is a thin, flaky brittle that you can use as a garnish or just have as a snack. My sprinkle blend of choice is a mixture of rainbow nonpareils and rainbow sprinkles. If you prefer different colors or like two different types of sprinkles together, use them—make it your own.

I enjoy the process of making the sprinkle brittle. This gives you a thin, crispy brittle—and it's really fun to lift it up when the chocolate hardens. Break it into whatever size pieces you want.

These two techniques for making chocolate brittle can be used with whatever additions you like. I recently made a "hummingbird" brittle with coconut and chopped pecans to decorate a hummingbird cake—it's also a delicious snack (and one of my mom's favorites).

MAKING CHOCOLATE DRIZZLE

You can make drizzle in the microwave, but I usually use a double boiler on the stove top because I'm working with larger quantities. It's very simple. Fill a saucepan with 1 or 2 inches of water and bring it to a boil, put a glass or other heat-safe bowl on top of it, fill it with the chocolate, and wait for it to melt. (I use compound chocolate, which you don't need to temper.) Once it melts, take the bowl out, and wipe off the bottom of the bowl to remove any excess water. (You don't want any water to get into the chocolate as it will affect the consistency.) Pour the melted chocolate into a disposable piping bag, snip the tip, and drizzle it on whatever you like.

DARK CHOCOLATE MUNCHIE BRITTLE

If you prefer a plain cake, this is also a delicious snack. If you're making a cake combination that is salty and sweet, topping it with munchie brittle is a great way to go.

3 cups dark chocolate melting wafers

1 cup crushed Cape Cod potato chips

1 cup crushed gluten-free pretzels

1 teaspoon fine sea salt

They're crunchier.

1. Tape two long pieces of wax paper or parchment to your table or countertop to create a workstation.

2. In a double boiler (or a metal bowl set over a pan of boiling water) melt the chocolate wafers, stirring until smooth.

3. Stir in the potato chips and pretzels, working quickly so that the chocolate doesn't begin to harden.

4. With a spatula, spread the chocolate mixture out on the wax paper and sprinkle the fine sea salt over the top.

5. Let harden for about 30 minutes, then break into pieces. Store in a covered container in the fridge to keep it crunchy. *OMG!*

WHITE CHOCOLATE MUNCHIE BRITTLE

Use white chocolate melting wafers instead of dark chocolate.

DARK OR WHITE CHOCOLATE CRUNCH

3 cups dark or white chocolate melting wafers

2 cups puffed quinoa

1. Tape two long pieces of wax paper or parchment to your table or countertop to create a workstation.

2. In a double boiler (or a metal bowl set over a pan of boiling water), melt the chocolate wafers, stirring until smooth.

3. Stir in the puffed quinoa, working quickly so that the chocolate doesn't begin to harden.

4. With a spatula, spread the chocolate mixture out on the wax paper.

5. Let harden for about 30 minutes, then break into pieces. Store in a covered container in the fridge to keep it crunchy.

ULTIMATE FLAVOR COMBOS (YUM!)

Read on . . .

This section is my personal gift to you. It represents how I actually create new flavor variations of existing product lines at Baked by Melissa. My first step is to write out the cake, filling, icing, and topping. I use these notes to organize my thoughts and then I go back and develop recipes. This book is my encouragement to you to be creative in your own right. Start with these basic notes, then go back into the book and look up the recipes. You'll be able to make the freshest, most delicious cakes and treats for the people you love.

S'MORES

CAKE: Grandma Annie's Chocolate Cake (page 89)

FILLINGS: Marshmallow Fluff and graham cracker pieces

ICING: Chocolate Icing (page 168)

TOPPINGS: Graham cracker pieces and marshmallows (and a sprinkle of coarse sea salt)

SAMOA

CAKE: Classic Vanilla Cake (page 34)

ICING: Chocolate Icing (page 168)

TOPPING: Coconut Goo (page 222)

CINNAMON BUN

CAKE: Cinnamon Cake (page 60)

ICING: Vanilla Glaze (page 218)

TOPPING: White chocolate drizzle (page 259)

PEANUT BUTTER BANANA

CAKE: Banana Cake (page 130)

ICING: Peanut Butter Cinnamon Icing (page 174)

TOPPING: Mini chocolate chips

CINNAMON PEANUT BUTTER

CAKE: Cinnamon Cake (page 60)

ICING: Peanut Butter Icing (page 174)

TOPPING: Coarse sea salt

PEANUT BUTTER AND JELLY

CAKE: Classic Vanilla Cake (page 34)

FILLING: Grape jelly

ICING: Real peanut butter

PEANUT BUTTER CUP

CAKE: Grandma Annie's Chocolate Cake (page 89)

FILLING: Real peanut butter

ICING: Chocolate Icing (page 168)

TOPPINGS: Real peanut butter and coarse sea salt

PEANUT BUTTER AND FLUFF

CAKE: Classic Vanilla Cake (page 34)

FILLING: Marshmallow Fluff

ICING: Peanut Butter Icing (page 174)

TOPPING: Coarse sea salt

LEMON

CAKE: Lemon Cake (page 56)

ICING: Lemon Icing (page 173)

TOPPING: Yellow sprinkles

LEMON MERINGUE PIE

CAKE: Lemon Cake (page 56)

ICING: Marshmallow Icing (page 184)

TOPPING: Graham cracker brittle

LEMON CHEESECAKE

CAKE: Lemon Cake (page 56)
FILLING: Cheesecake Icing (page 192)
ICING: Cream Cheese Icing (page 185)
TOPPING: Graham Cracker Crumble (page 242)

LEMON BLUEBERRY

CAKE: Grandma Sylvia's Blueberry Cake (page 58)
ICING: Lemon Icing (page 173)
TOPPINGS: Grated lemon zest and fresh blueberries

LEMON STRAWBERRY

CAKE: Lemon Cake (page 56)
ICING: Strawberry Icing (page 172)
TOPPINGS: Grated lemon zest and fresh strawberries

BLUEBERRY

CAKE: Grandma Sylvia's Blueberry Cake (page 58)
ICING: Vanilla Glaze (page 218)

BLUEBERRIES AND CREAM

CAKE: Grandma Sylvia's Blueberry Cake (page 58)
ICING: Vanilla Icing (page 161)
TOPPING: Fresh blueberries

BLUEBERRY CHEESECAKE

CAKE: Grandma Sylvia's Blueberry Cake (page 58)
FILLING: Blueberry preserves
ICING: Cheesecake Icing (page 192)
TOPPING: Graham Cracker Crumble (page 242)

COFFEE CAKE

CAKE: Classic Vanilla Cake (page 34)
TOPPINGS: Shortbread Crumble (page 243) baked in and white chocolate drizzle (page 259)

CHOCOLATE COFFEE CAKE

CAKE: Grandma Annie's Chocolate Espresso Cake (page 98)
TOPPINGS: Shortbread Crumble (page 242) baked in and white chocolate drizzle (page 259)

CINNAMON COFFEE CAKE

CAKE: Cinnamon Cake (page 60)
TOPPINGS: Cinnamon Crumble (page 242) baked in and white chocolate drizzle (page 259)

COOKIES AND CREAM

CAKE: Grandma Annie's Chocolate Cake (page 89)
FILLING: Cookies and Cream Icing (page 176)
ICING: Vanilla Icing (page 161)
TOPPING: Oreo Cookies

COOKIE DOUGH

CAKE: Classic Vanilla Cake (page 34)
FILLING: Sugar Cookie Dough Icing (page 175)
ICING: Chocolate Icing (page 168)
TOPPING: Sugar Cookie Dough Topping (page 244)

DECONSTRUCTED COOKIE DOUGH

CAKE: Classic Vanilla Cake (page 34)
FILLING: Sugar Cookie Dough Icing (page 175)
ICING: Chocolate Icing (page 168)
TOPPING: Rainbow sprinkles and mini chocolate chips

COOKIES AND MILK

CAKE: Classic Vanilla Cake (page 34) with (store-bought) cookie dough baked in
FILLING: Sugar Cookie Dough Icing (page 175)
ICING: Hot Cocoa Icing (page 186)
TOPPING: Sugar Cookie Dough Topping (page 244)

COOKIES AND CHOCOLATE MILK

CAKE: Grandma Annie's Chocolate Cake (page 89) with (store-bought) cookie dough baked in

FILLING: Sugar Cookie Dough Icing (page 175)

ICING: Hot Cocoa Icing (page 186)

TOPPING: Sugar Cookie Dough Topping (page 244)

COCONUT

CAKE: Coconut Cake (page 148)

FILLING: Coconut Icing (page 203)

ICING: Vanilla Icing (page 161)

TOPPINGS: Toasted coconut and shredded coconut–white chocolate brittle

CHOCOLATE COCONUT

CAKE: Coconut Cake (page 148)

FILLING: Coconut Icing (page 203)

ICING: Vanilla Icing (page 161)

TOPPING: Toasted coconut and shredded coconut–dark chocolate brittle

MOUNDS

CAKE: Classic Vanilla Cake (page 34)

FILLING: Coconut Icing (page 203)

ICING: Chocolate Icing (page 168)

TOPPING: Unsweetened shredded coconut

TIE-DYE

CAKE: Classic Vanilla Cake (page 37)

FILLING: Vanilla Icing (page 161)

ICING: Vanilla Icing (page 161)

GLAZE: Vanilla Glaze (page 218)

TOPPINGS: Rainbow sprinkles, nonpareils, and white chocolate rainbow brittle

CHOCOLATE TIE-DYE

CAKE: The Tie-Dye Cake (page 37)

ICING: Chocolate Icing (page 168)

TOPPINGS: Rainbow sprinkles, nonpareils, and white chocolate rainbow brittle

MINT CHOCOLATE COOKIE

CAKE: Grandma Annie's Chocolate Cake (page 89)

ICING: Cookies and Cream Icing (page 176) with Thin Mints

TOPPINGS: Mint cookie crumble and green chocolate drizzle (see page 259)

MINT CHOCOLATE CHIP

CAKE: Mint Leaf Cake (page 155)

FILLING: Chocolate fudge sauce

ICING: Chocolate Icing (page 168) or Real Mint Icing (page 198)

DOUBLE COOKIE

CAKE: Grandma Annie's Chocolate Cake (page 89)

FILLING: Sugar Cookie Dough Icing (page 175)

ICING: Cookies and Cream Icing (page 176)

TOPPING: Sugar Cookie Dough Topping (page 244) and Oreo pieces

SUGAR COOKIE DOUGH

CAKE: Classic Vanilla Cake (page 34)

ICING: Sugar Cookie Dough Icing (page 175)

TOPPINGS: Sugar Cookie Dough Topping (page 244) and white chocolate rainbow nonpareils brittle

SUGAR COOKIE CHEESECAKE

CAKE: Classic Vanilla Cake (page 34)

FILLING: Cheesecake Icing (page 192)

ICING: Sugar Cookie Dough Icing (page 175)

TOPPING: White chocolate rainbow brittle

SNICKERDOODLE

CAKE: Cinnamon Cake (page 60)

ICING: Sugar Cookie Dough Icing (page 175)

TOPPING: Cinnamon sprinkle

CHOCOLATE CHIP SUGAR COOKIE

CAKE: Chocolate Chip Cake (page 62)

ICING: Sugar Cookie Dough Icing (page 175)

TOPPING: Mini chocolate chips

NUTELLA SUGAR COOKIE

CAKE: Hot Cocoa Cake (page 71)

FILLING: Sugar Cookie Dough Icing (page 175)

ICING: Nutella Icing (page 190)

TOPPING: Sugar Cookie Dough Topping (page 244) and dark chocolate drizzle (page 259)

CHOCOLATE CHEESECAKE

CAKE: Grandma Annie's Chocolate Cake (page 89)

FILLING: Chocolate Cheesecake Icing (page 193)

ICING: Chocolate Cream Cheese Icing (page 185)

TOPPING: Oreo Crumble (page 242)

PEANUT BUTTER CHEESECAKE

CAKE: Peanut Butter Cake (page 116)

FILLING: Cheesecake Icing (page 192)

ICING: Peanut Butter Cream Cheese Icing (page 185)

TOPPING: Coarse sea salt

DULCE DE LECHE

CAKE: Dulce de Leche Cake (page 82)

ICING: Dulce de Leche Icing (page 183)

TOPPING: Coarse sea salt

CHOCOLATE CARAMEL

CAKE: Grandma Annie's Chocolate Cake (page 89)

FILLING: Dulce de Leche Icing (page 183)

ICING: Dulce de Leche Icing (page 183)

TOPPINGS: Dark chocolate drizzle (page 259) and coarse sea salt

CARAMEL FUDGE

CAKE: Dulce de Leche Cake (page 82)

FILLING: Chocolate fudge sauce

ICING: Dulce de Leche Icing (page 183)

TOPPING: Salted dark chocolate brittle

TRIPLE CHOCOLATE FUDGE

CAKE: Grandma Annie's Chocolate Cake (page 89)

FILLING: Chocolate fudge sauce

ICING: Chocolate Icing (page 168)

TOPPINGS: Oreo Crumble (page 242) and coarse sea salt

CHOCOLATE CHOCOLATE CHIP

CAKE: Chocolate Chip Cake (page 62)

ICING: Chocolate Icing (page 168)

TOPPING: Mini chocolate chips

PEANUT BUTTER CHOCOLATE CHIP

CAKE: Peanut Butter Cake (page 116)

ICING: Peanut Butter Icing (page 174)

TOPPING: Mini chocolate chips

Add chocolate chips to the batter!

CHOCOLATE MARSHMALLOW

CAKE: Grandma Annie's Chocolate Cake (page 89)

FILLING: Marshmallow Fluff (overstuffed)

ICING: Chocolate Icing (page 168)

TOPPING: Mini marshmallows

MARSHMALLOW
CAKE: Classic Vanilla Cake (page 34)
FILLING: Marshmallow Fluff (overstuffed)
ICING: Vanilla Icing (page 161)
TOPPING: Mini marshmallows

RAINBOW COOKIE
CAKE: Almond Cake (page 104)
FILLING: Strawberry or apricot jam
ICING: Chocolate Icing (page 168)
TOPPING: Pink, yellow, and green sprinkles

CARAMEL COFFEE
CAKE: Grandma Annie's Chocolate Espresso Cake (page 98)
ICING: Chocolate Espresso Icing (page 177)
TOPPING: Coarse sea salt

ESPRESSO FUDGE
CAKE: Grandma Annie's Chocolate Espresso Cake (page 98)
FILLING: Chocolate fudge sauce (overstuffed)
ICING: Chocolate Espresso Icing (page 177)
TOPPING: Dark chocolate drizzle (page 259)

ESPRESSO CHIP
CAKE: Grandma Annie's Chocolate Espresso Cake (page 98)
ICING: Chocolate Espresso Icing (page 177)
TOPPING: Mini chocolate chips

ESPRESSO
CAKE: Grandma Annie's Chocolate Espresso Cake (page 98)
ICING: Chocolate Espresso Icing (page 177)

ESPRESSO CREAM
CAKE: Grandma Annie's Chocolate Espresso Cake (page 98)
ICING: Vanilla Icing (page 161)

MOCHA CHIP
CAKE: Grandma Annie's Chocolate Espresso Cake (page 98)
ICING: Chocolate Icing (page 168)
TOPPING: Chocolate chips

BOSTON CREAM
CAKE: Classic Vanilla Cake (page 34)
FILLING: Instant vanilla pudding
ICING: Chocolate Icing (page 168)
TOPPING: White chocolate drizzle (page 259)

NEW YORK CREAM
CAKE: Classic Vanilla Cake (page 34)
FILLING: Instant vanilla pudding
ICING: Chocolate Icing (page 168)
TOPPING: Dark chocolate drizzle (page 259)

CANNOLI
CAKE: Classic Vanilla Cake (page 34)
FILLING: Cannoli cream
TOPPINGS: Cannoli shells and chocolate chips

CHOCOLATE CANNOLI
CAKE: Grandma Annie's Chocolate Cake (page 89)
FILLING: Cannoli cream
TOPPINGS: Cannoli shells and chocolate chips

NUTELLA
CAKE: Classic Vanilla Cake (page 34)
ICING: Nutella

NUTELLA CHIP

CAKE: Chocolate Chip Cake (page 62)

ICING: Nutella

TOPPING: Chocolate chips

MARBLE CHIP

CAKE: Marble or one layer Grandma Annie's Chocolate Cake (page 89) and one layer Classic Vanilla Cake (page 34)

swirl these! →

ICING: Chocolate Icing (page 168) and Vanilla Icing (page 161)

TOPPING: Chocolate chips

PUMPKIN

CAKE: Pumpkin Spice Cake (page 126)

ICING: Cream Cheese Icing (page 185)

TOPPING: Orange sprinkles

PUMPKIN SPICE

CAKE: Pumpkin Spice Cake (page 126)

ICING: Cream Cheese Icing (page 185)

TOPPINGS: Orange sprinkles and pumpkin pie spice

PUMPKIN SPICE LATTE

CAKE: Pumpkin Spice Latte Cake (page 127)

ICING: Espresso Icing (page 177)

TOPPING: Orange sprinkles and pumpkin pie spice

PEANUT BUTTER

CAKE: Peanut Butter Cake (page 116)

FILLING: Real peanut butter

ICING: Peanut Butter Icing (page 174)

PEANUT BUTTER CINNAMON

CAKE: Peanut Butter Cake (page 116)

ICING: Cinnamon Icing (page 171)

TOPPING: Reese's Pieces

SOOO BAKED

CAKE: Grandma Annie's Chocolate Cake (page 89)

FILLING: Chocolate Chip Cookie Dough Icing (page 178)

ICING: Chocolate Icing (page 168) and Vanilla Icing (page 161)

Swirl these! ←

TOPPING: Brownie pieces

RED VELVET

CAKE: Red Velvet Cake (page 154)

ICING: Cream Cheese Icing (page 185)

TOPPING: Red sugar crystals

CHOCOLATE RED VELVET

CAKE: Red Velvet Cake (page 154)

ICING: Chocolate Cream Cheese Icing (page 185)

TOPPING: Red sugar crystals or Red Velvet Cake crumbs

CINNAMON

CAKE: Cinnamon Cake (page 60)

FILLING: Cinnamon Icing (page 171)

ICING: Cinnamon Icing (page 171)

CHOCOLATE CHIP PANCAKE

CAKE: Pancake Cake (page 144)

ICING: Maple Icing (page 189)

TOPPING: Mini chocolate chips

BLUEBERRY PANCAKE

CAKE: Pancake Cake (page 144)

ICING: Maple Icing (page 189)

TOPPING: Fresh blueberries

CHOCOLATE BANANA

CAKE: Banana Cake (page 130)

ICING: Chocolate Icing (page 168)

SUNDAE

CAKE: Grandma Annie's Chocolate Cake (page 89)

FILLING: Dulce de Leche Icing (page 183)

ICING: Vanilla Icing (page 161)

TOPPINGS: Rainbow sprinkles, maraschino cherries, and dark chocolate drizzle (page 259)

BANANA CAKE

CAKE: Banana Cake (page 130) ← *Add nuts to the batter!*

ICING: Cream Cheese Icing (page 185)

TOPPING: Chocolate pecan brittle

BLUEBERRY BANANA

CAKE: Grandma Sylvia's Blueberry Banana Cake (page 58)

ICING: Cream Cheese Icing (page 185)

TOPPING: Fresh blueberries

HUMMINGBIRD

CAKE: Hummingbird Cake (page 112)

ICING: Cream Cheese Icing (page 185)

TOPPING: Hummingbird brittle (page 255)

BIRTHDAY CAKE

CAKE: Classic Vanilla Cake (page 34)

ICING: Chocolate Icing (page 168)

TOPPING: Rainbow sprinkles

STRAWBERRY

CAKE: Strawberry Cake (page 55)

ICING: Strawberry Icing (page 172)

TOPPING: Fresh strawberries

CHOCOLATE STRAWBERRY

CAKE: Strawberry Cake (page 55)

ICING: Chocolate Icing (page 168)

TOPPING: Fresh strawberries

BERRY

CAKE: One layer Strawberry Cake (page 55) and one layer Grandma Sylvia's Blueberry Cake (page 58)

ICING: Cream Cheese Icing (page 185)

TOPPING: Fresh strawberries and blueberries

NEAPOLITAN

CAKE: Strawberry Cake (page 55)

FILLING: Chocolate fudge

ICING: Vanilla Icing (page 161)

TOPPING: Pink sprinkles

STRAWBERRY SHORTCAKE

CAKE: Strawberry Cake (page 55)

ICING: Vanilla Icing (page 161)

FILLINGS: Fresh strawberries and Shortbread Crumble (page 243)

LEMON NANA

CAKE: Lemon Cake (page 56)

ICING: Real Mint Icing (page 198)

TOPPING: Mint leaves

PRETZEL CRUNCH

CAKE: Classic Vanilla Cake (page 34)

ICING: Vanilla Icing (page 161) with pretzels

TOPPING: White chocolate pretzel brittle (page 255)

WEDDING CAKE

CAKE: Classic Vanilla Cake (page 34)

ICING: Vanilla Icing (page 161)

TOPPING: White chocolate shavings and white sugar crystals

FRUITY PEBBLES

CAKE: Cereal Cake (page 79)

ICING: Vanilla Icing (page 161)

TOPPING: Fruity Pebble brittle

GOLDEN GRAHAMS AND MILK

CAKE: Cereal Cake (page 79) made with Golden Grahams cereal

ICING: Cereal Icing (page 196) made with Golden Grahams

TOPPING: Golden Grahams and white chocolate drizzle (page 259)

CRAZY CEREAL

CAKE: One layer Cereal Cake (page 79) made with Fruity Pebbles and one layer made with Golden Grahams cereal

ICING: Cereal Icing (page 196) made with Cocoa Puffs cereal

TOPPINGS: Cocoa Puffs, Fruity Pebbles, and Golden Grahams

VANILLA COOKIES AND CREAM

CAKE: Classic Vanilla Cake (page 34)

ICING: Cookies and Cream Icing (page 176)

TOPPING: Oreo pieces

CARROT CAKE

CAKE: Carrot Cake (page 142)

ICING: Cream Cheese Icing (page 185)

TOPPINGS: Mini chocolate chips and orange sprinkle brittle

GREEN TEA

CAKE: Matcha Cake (page 84)

ICING: Matcha Icing (page 188) or Matcha Glaze (page 235)

CREAM CHEESE AND JAM

CAKE: Classic Vanilla Cake (page 34)

FILLING: Strawberry jam

ICING: Cream Cheese Icing (page 185)

CANDY CANE CRUNCH

CAKE: Classic Vanilla Cake (page 34)

FILLING: Vanilla Icing (page 161)

ICING: Vanilla Icing (page 161)

TOPPING: White chocolate candy cane brittle

CHOCOLATE CANDY CANE CRUNCH

CAKE: Grandma Annie's Chocolate Cake (page 89)

FILLING: Chocolate Icing (page 168)

ICING: Chocolate Icing (page 168)

TOPPING: Dark chocolate candy cane brittle (page 255)

CHOCOLATE TOFFEE CRUNCH

CAKE: Grandma Annie's Chocolate Cake (page 89)

FILLING: Dulce de Leche Icing (page 183) with toffee pieces

ICING: Chocolate Icing (page 168)

TOPPING: Toffee crunch brittle

VANILLA LATTE

CAKE: Classic Vanilla Cake (page 34)

ICING: Espresso Icing (page 177)

TOPPING: White Chocolate Munchie Brittle (page 262)

BANANA PUDDING

CAKE: Banana Cake (page 130)

FILLING: Instant vanilla pudding

ICING: Vanilla Icing (page 161)

TOPPING: Coarse sea salt

CORNBREAD

CAKE: Cornbread Cake (page 152)

ICING: Cream Cheese Icing (page 185)

TOPPING: Yellow nonpareils

SNO CAP

CAKE: Grandma Annie's Chocolate Cake (page 89)

FILLING: Marshmallow Icing (page 184)

ICING: Chocolate Icing (page 168)

TOPPING: White nonpareils to cover the cake

CHOCOLATE MAPLE

CAKE: Grandma Annie's Chocolate Cake (page 89)

ICING: Maple Icing (page 189)

DOUGHNUT

CAKE: Doughnut Cake (page 66)

ICING: Doughnut Icing (page 170)

TOPPING: Doughnut cake crumble

JELLY DOUGHNUT

CAKE: Doughnut Cake (page 66)

FILLING: Strawberry jam

ICING: Doughnut Icing (page 170)

TOPPING: Confectioners' sugar

CHOCOLATE GLAZED DOUGHNUT

CAKE: Doughnut Cake (page 66)

ICING: Chocolate Glaze (page 222)

TOPPING: Rainbow nonpareils

GLAZED DOUGHNUT

CAKE: Doughnut Cake (page 66)

ICING: Vanilla Glaze (page 218)

TOPPING: Rainbow nonpareils

CHOCOLATE RASPBERRY

CAKE: Grandma Annie's Chocolate Cake (page 89)

FILLING: Raspberry jam

ICING: Chocolate Icing (page 168)

TOPPING: Fresh raspberries

HOT COCOA

CAKE: Hot Cocoa Cake (page 71)

FILLING: Marshmallow Fluff

ICING: Hot Cocoa Icing (page 186)

TOPPING: Mini marshmallows

PEPPERMINT HOT COCOA

CAKE: Grandma Annie's Chocolate Cake (page 89) or Hot Cocoa Cake (page 71)

FILLING: Marshmallow Fluff

ICING: Peppermint chocolate

TOPPINGS: Dark chocolate candy cane brittle and white chocolate drizzle

CLASSIC CAKE WITH BERRIES

CAKE: Classic Vanilla Cake (page 34)

ICING: Whipped Vanilla Icing (page 204)

TOPPING: Fresh berries

CLASSIC PB&J

CAKE: Classic Vanilla Cake (page 34)

FILLING: Grape jam

ICING: Real peanut butter

MATCHA LATTE

CAKE: Matcha Cake (page 84)

ICING: Whipped Vanilla Icing (page 204)

TOPPING: Sifted matcha powder

CANDY BAR

CAKE: Classic Vanilla Cake (page 34)

FILLING: Dulce de Leche Icing (page 183)

ICING: Chocolate Icing (page 168)

TOPPING: Candy bar pieces of your choice

STRAWBERRY CRUMB

CAKE: Strawberry Cake (page 55)

TOPPING: Shortbread Crumble (page 243) baked in

BLUEBERRY CRUMB

CAKE: Grandma Sylvia's Blueberry Cake (page 58)

TOPPING: Shortbread Crumble (page 243) baked in

CEREAL CRUMB

CAKE: Cereal Cake (page 79)

TOPPING: Cereal Crumble (page 243) baked in

TRIPLE CHOCOLATE CRUMB

CAKE: Grandma Annie's Chocolate Cake (page 89)

TOPPINGS: Chocolate Crumble (page 243) baked in, dark chocolate drizzle (page 259), and rainbow nonpareils

MATCHA BUNDT CAKE

CAKE: Matcha Cake (page 84)

ICING: Vanilla Glaze (page 218)

TOPPING: Sifted matcha green tea powder

PEANUT BUTTER CHOCOLATE BUNDT

CAKE: Peanut Butter Cake (page 116)

ICING: Chocolate Glaze (page 222)

TOPPING: Coarse sea salt

PANCAKE BUNDT

CAKE: Pancake Cake (page 144)

ICING: Maple Glaze (page 235)

PEANUT BUTTER BUNDT

CAKE: Peanut Butter Cake (page 116)

ICING: Cinnamon Glaze (page 229)

TOPPING: Coarse sea salt

PUMPKIN BUNDT

CAKE: Pumpkin Spice Cake (page 128)

ICING: Pumpkin Spice Glaze (page 230)

STRAWBERRY SUGAR COOKIE

CAKE: Strawberry Cake (page 55)

ICING: Sugar Cookie Dough Icing (page 175)

TOPPING: Shortbread Crumble (page 243)

CAKE BATTER

CAKE: Classic Vanilla Cake (page 34)

ICING: Cake Batter Icing (page 199)

TOPPING: Rainbow sprinkles

BROWNIE BATTER

CAKE: Grandma Annie's Chocolate Cake (page 89)

ICING: Brownie Batter Icing (page 202)

TOPPING: Brownie pieces

SLUTTY CAKE

CAKE: Classic Vanilla Cake (page 34) with cookie dough baked in

FILLING: Cheesecake Icing (page 192)

ICING: Brownie Batter Icing (page 202)

TOPPING: Chocolate Chip Cookie Dough Topping (page 244), Oreo pieces

SALTED CARAMEL HOT CHOCOLATE

CAKE: Hot Cocoa Cake (page 71)

FILLING: Salted Caramel Icing (page 183)

ICING: Hot Cocoa Icing (page 186)

TOPPING: Mini marshmallows

HINT OF CINNAMON

CAKE: Classic Vanilla Cake (page 34)

ICING: Cinnamon Icing (page 171)

CHOCO-VANILLA

CAKE: Grandma Annie's Chocolate Cake (page 89)

ICING: Vanilla Icing (page 161)

TOPPING: Rainbow sprinkles and white chocolate brittle

CHOCO BUNDT

CAKE: Grandma Annie's Chocolate Cake (page 89)

ICING: Vanilla Glaze (page 218)

TOPPING: Coarse sea salt

CHOCOLATE BABKA

CAKE: Grandma Annie's Chocolate Cake (page 89)

FILLING: Cinnamon Icing (page 171)

ICING: Chocolate Icing (page 168)

TOPPINGS: Cinnamon Crumble (page 242) and dark chocolate drizzle (page 259)

HOT COCOA PEANUT BUTTER

CAKE: Hot Cocoa Cake (page 71)

FILLING: Peanut Butter Icing (page 174)

ICING: Hot Cocoa Icing (page 186)

TOPPINGS: Mini marshmallows and drizzled peanut butter

SCOTTIE'S SMASH CAKE

CAKE: One layer Grandma Annie's Chocolate Cake (page 89), one layer Peanut Butter Cake (page 116), and one layer Classic Vanilla Cake (page 34)

FILLING: Peanut Butter Icing (page 174) and Hot Cocoa Icing (page 186)

ICING: Sugar Cookie Dough Icing (page 175)

TOPPINGS: Rainbow sprinkles, nonpareils, and pink glaze drip

TIRAMISU

CAKE: Grandma Annie's Chocolate Espresso Cake (page 98)

ICING: Cheesecake Icing (page 192)

TOPPING: Unsweetened cocoa powder

Share your creations with me!
@bakedbymelissa
@melissabenishay
#cakesbymelissa

CAKE

CAKE: _____

FILLING: _____

ICING: _____

GLAZE: _____

TOPPING: _____

CAKE

CAKE: _____

FILLING: _____

ICING: _____

GLAZE: _____

TOPPING: _____

CAKE

CAKE: _____

FILLING: _____

ICING: _____

GLAZE: _____

TOPPING: _____

CAKE

CAKE: _____

FILLING: _____

ICING: _____

GLAZE: _____

TOPPING: _____

CAKE

CAKE: _____

FILLING: _____

ICING: _____

GLAZE: _____

TOPPING: _____

CAKE

CAKE: _____

FILLING: _____

ICING: _____

GLAZE: _____

TOPPING: _____

CAKE

CAKE: _____

FILLING: _____

ICING: _____

GLAZE: _____

TOPPING: _____

CAKE

CAKE: _____

FILLING: _____

ICING: _____

GLAZE: _____

TOPPING: _____

CAKE

CAKE: _____

FILLING: _____

ICING: _____

GLAZE: _____

TOPPING: _____

CAKE

CAKE: _____

FILLING: _____

ICING: _____

GLAZE: _____

TOPPING: _____

CAKE

CAKE: _____

FILLING: _____

ICING: _____

GLAZE: _____

TOPPING: _____

CAKE

CAKE: _____

FILLING: _____

ICING: _____

GLAZE: _____

TOPPING: _____

CAKE

CAKE: _____

FILLING: _____

ICING: _____

GLAZE: _____

TOPPING: _____

CAKE

CAKE: _____

FILLING: _____

ICING: _____

GLAZE: _____

TOPPING: _____

ACKNOWLEDGMENTS

• •

Every day I get asked how I do it all. It's such bullshit because I *don't* do it all. I have an amazing team working with me at Baked by Melissa and that's how we've grown and that's how we'll continue to grow. The same is true for this book: I never use the word *blessed* because I think it's such a cliché, but I've been blessed with a magical team of people. I've had the time of my life working on this book. We've brought together a group of people who are passionate and like-minded, hard-working, and super-creative and that's the recipe for success.

None of this would be possible without my family: My husband, Adi, who stepped in and picked up our daughter, Scottie, at school every day when I was working late in the test kitchen or at photo shoots. My parents and my brother have told me I could do anything and have been my biggest fans every single day of my entire life—more so now than ever before. Without them, I wouldn't be here writing this book. I'm a product of the people I surround myself with, and my family is a big part of that.

My tie-dye family at Baked by Melissa: Seth Horowitz, our leader, whose energy is so overwhelmingly positive and encouraging. We have a magical partnership, and I can't wait to see where it goes. Taylor Block, communications manager at Baked by Melissa, served as project manager for this book and organized everything from shooting locations to paperwork so that I could do what I'm good at, which is bake and develop recipes and create. I couldn't have made this book without her. My Baked by Melissa team, who supported me throughout this process, acted as the best taste-testing team I know and helped me to develop the most delicious recipes for all of you to create yourselves at home. More specifically, my wonderful brand and creative team at Baked by Melissa, especially Lisa Bondi and Veronica Clauss, who designed the cover of the book and do everything every day so effortlessly and in no time at all, and Victoria Spektor, our head of marketing.

My agent, Jennifer Cohen, who led us to HarperCollins, and the entire publishing team at William Morrow, especially Lisa Sharkey, senior vice president and director of creative development, for being so open to having me write a book and telling me I could do whatever I wanted with it, and Alieza Schvimer, associate editor, for guiding us so thoughtfully through the publishing process. Liate Stehlik, publisher; Suet Chong and Mumtaz Mustafa, designers; Rachel Meyers, production editor; Katherine Turro and Tavia Kowalchuk, marketing; and Katie Steinberg, publicity: Thank you for being so open to letting my freak flag fly and allowing me to do this book in a way that rings true to me, Baked by Melissa, and, most important, to my creative process, which I've tried to showcase here.

I found a soul mate in photographer Ashley Sears, and that doesn't happen very often. She is hard-working, free-spirited, wildly creative, and just an all-around good person. It's not so easy to trust someone else with your baby. With Ashley, it was like we shared the same brain as well as the same creative vision. Without her, this book wouldn't be as amazing as it is.

My equally amazing writer, Marisa Bulzone, who really understood my vision from day one. Together, we concocted this wonderful book that is who I am, and I owe it to you, Marisa. It was so enjoyable to work with you.

Gene Monaco was my baking assistant through the whole process. Working with him was so fun and effortless; in the kitchen and on set, he helped so much and added so much to the project.

Julia Choi, our food stylist, is my polar opposite but we really complemented each other. She has such a neat way about her, and she let me be my creative, messy self. I learned a lot from her, too.

Juliya Madorskaya, our culinary assistant, was so helpful. Our photography team—Simon Lewis, lead assistant; Lauren Damaskinos, second assistant; Jameson Zakora; and Nitzan Rubin; along with props styling assistants Michael Altman and Christian Galuppi—made the photo shoots so much fun. Special thanks to hair stylist Jaquel Jones of Versatility Is Key and makeup artist Jane Meng of 25th and Jane for making me look great.

The Studio at One Kings Lane in New York City served as our lifestyle set for the photo shoots. Their team was so fun and accommodating; our shoot days with them will be remembered forever. Props for the photos were provided by Felt+Fat, Surface Workshop, and GreenLife.

UNIVERSAL CONVERSION CHART

OVEN TEMPERATURE EQUIVALENTS

250°F = 120°C	350°F = 180°C	450°F = 230°C
275°F = 135°C	375°F = 190°C	475°F = 240°C
300°F = 150°C	400°F = 200°C	500°F = 260°C
325°F = 160°C	425°F = 220°C	

MEASUREMENT EQUIVALENTS

Measurements should always be level unless directed otherwise.

⅛ teaspoon = 0.5 mL

¼ teaspoon = 1 mL

½ teaspoon = 2 mL

1 teaspoon = 5 mL

1 tablespoon = 3 teaspoons = ½ fluid ounce = 15 mL

2 tablespoons = ⅛ cup = 1 fluid ounce = 30 mL

4 tablespoons = ¼ cup = 2 fluid ounces = 60 mL

5⅓ tablespoons = ⅓ cup = 3 fluid ounces = 80 mL

8 tablespoons = ½ cup = 4 fluid ounces = 120 mL

10⅔ tablespoons = ⅔ cup = 5 fluid ounces = 160 mL

12 tablespoons = ¾ cup = 6 fluid ounces = 180 mL

16 tablespoons = 1 cup = 8 fluid ounces = 240 mL

INDEX

Note: Page references in *italics* indicate photographs.

A

Almond
  Cake, 104–5
  Rainbow Cookie Cake, *106,*
    107–8, 109–11

B

Banana(s)
  Cake, 130–31
  Cake Loaves, Mini, 132–33,
    132–33
  Cake with Peanut Butter, *136,*
    137–38, 139–40
  Chocolate Chip Cake, 131
  Everything But the Kitchen Sink
    Muffins, *134,* 135
  Hummingbird Cake, 112–13
  Hummingbird Cupcakes, *114,*
    115
  Pancake Cake, 144–45
  ripening, 131
  Scottie's Smash Cake, 120–23,
    121–22
Bench scraper, 22
Berry(ies). *See also* Blueberry(ies);
    Strawberry
  Cake, *210,* 211, *212–13*
Birthday Cake, Classic, 169, *169*
Blueberry(ies)
  Cake, Grandma Sylvia's, 58–59
  Everything But the Kitchen Sink
    Muffins, *134,* 135

Mini Banana Cake Loaves,
  132–33, *132–33*
Pancake Cake, 144–45
Bowls, 19
Brittle
  Dark Chocolate Munchie, 262
  Hummingbird, *114,* 115
  making, 255
  White Chocolate Munchie,
    262
Brownies and brownie mix
  Brownie Batter Icing, 202
  buying mixes for recipes, 25
  Slutty Cake, *248,* 249–52,
    250–51, 253
Brown Sugar
  Cake, 50–51
  storing, 24
Butter, for recipes, 24
Buttermilk, about, 25

C

Cake Batter Icing, 199
Cake cutters, 21
Cake pans, 19–20
Cake rounds
  cardboard, 21
  parchment and wax, 20
Cakes (basic)
  Almond, 104–5
  Banana, 130–31
  Banana Chocolate Chip, 131

Blueberry, Grandma Sylvia's,
  58–59
Brown Sugar, 50–51
Carrot, 142–43
Cereal, 79
Chocolate, Grandma Annie's, 89
Chocolate Chip, 62–63
Chocolate Chip Carrot, 143
Chocolate Espresso, Grandma
  Annie's, 98
Cinnamon, 60–61
Coconut, 148–49
Coffee, 88
Cornbread, 152–53, *153*
Doughnut, 66–67
Dulce de Leche, 82–83
Funfetti, 78
Hot Cocoa, 68–69
Hummingbird, 112–13
Lemon, 56
Matcha, 84
Mint Leaf, 155
Pancake, 144–45
Peanut Butter, 116–17
Pumpkin Spice, 126–27
Pumpkin Spice Latte, 127
Red Velvet, 154
Strawberry, 52–53
Vanilla, Classic, 34–35
Cakes (decorated). *See also*
    Cupcakes
  Banana, Loaves, Mini, 132–33,
    132–33

Cakes (*cont.*)
  Banana, with Peanut Butter,
    136, 137–38, *139–40*
  Berry, *210*, 211, *212–13*
  Birthday, Classic, 169, *169*
  Cake Doughnuts, *220*, 221
  The Cereal Cake, *80*, 81
  Chocolate Chip Loaf, 64, *65*
  Chocolate Espresso Crumble,
    99, 100–101, *102–3*
  Chocolate Peanut Butter, *90*, 91
  Coconut, The, *150*, 151
  Cookies and Cream, *166*, 167
  The Double Cookie, *179–80*,
    181
  Hot Cocoa, *70*, 71–72, *73–77*
  Limonana, 57, *57*
  Matcha, 85, *86–87*
  Neapolitan, 92, *93*
  Pancake, Ice Cream Sandwiches
    with, 146, *147*
  Pumpkin Spice, 128, *129*
  Pumpkin Spice Latte, 128, *129*
  Rainbow Cookie, *106*, 107–8,
    109–11
  Samoa Doughnuts, *224*,
    225–26, *227*
  Scottie's Smash, 120–23, *121–22*
  Slutty, *248*, 249–52, *250–51*,
    253
  Strawberry, *54*, 55
  The Tie-Dye, *36*, *37–42*
  ultimate flavor combinations,
    266–76
  Vanilla, with Sugar Cookie
    Dough, 48–49, *49*
Cakes (general information)
  baking times, 31
  baking tips, 26–27
  cutting into layers, 21
  equipment and tools for, 19–22
  making waffles with batter, 29
  pan sizes and recipe yields, 31

pantry items for, 24–25
round top, leveling, 21
servings per cake, 30
testing for doneness, 30
Cake turntable, 21
Canisters for flour and sugar, 21
Caramel
  Chocolate Espresso Crumble
    Cake, 99, 100–101, *102–3*
  Coffee Icing, 191
  Glaze, 236
  Salted, Glaze, 236
  Salted, Icing, 183
  Salted, Icing, Whipped, 207
  Samoa Doughnuts, *224*,
    225–26, *227*
Cardboard cake rounds, 21
Carrot
  Cake, 142–43
  Chocolate Chip Cake, 143
Cereal
  Cake, 79
  Cake, The, *80*, 81
  Cake Doughnuts, *220*, 221
  Crumble, 243, *243*
  Icing, 196
Cheese. *See* Cream Cheese
Cheesecake Icing, 192
  Chocolate, 193
  Cinnamon, 193
  Peanut Butter, 193
  Peanut Butter Cinnamon, 193
  Strawberry, 193
Chocolate. *See also* Chocolate
    Chip Cookie Dough; Hot
    cocoa; Nutella; Oreo cookies;
    White Chocolate
  baker's, about, 24
  Brownie Batter Icing, 202
  Cake, Grandma Annie's, 89
  Cake Doughnuts, *220*, 221
  Cheesecake Icing, 193
  Chip Banana Cake, 131

Chip Cake, 62–63
Chip Carrot Cake, 143
Chip Loaf Cake, 64, *65*
chips, micro, about, 24
Classic Birthday Cake, 169,
  169
Cookies and Cream Cake, *166*,
  167
Cookies and Cream Cupcake,
  164, *165*
Cookies and Cream Icing, 176
Cream Cheese Icing, 185
Crumble, 243, *243*
Dark, Crunch, 263, *263*
Dark, Munchie Brittle, 262
The Double Cookie Cake,
  179–80, 181
drizzle, making, 259
Espresso Cake, Grandma
  Annie's, 98
Espresso Crumble Cake, *99*,
  100–101, *102–3*
Espresso Icing, 177
Everything But the Kitchen Sink
  Muffins, *134*, 135
Glaze, 222, *223*
Hot Cocoa Cupcakes, 187,
  187
Ice Cream Sandwiches with
  Pancake Cake, 146, *147*
Icing, 168, *169*
Icing, Whipped, 204
Mini Banana Cake Loaves,
  132–33, *132–33*
Neapolitan Cake, 92, *93*
Pancake Cake, 144–45
Peanut Butter Cake, *90*, 91
Peanut Butter Cup Cupcakes,
  90, 91
Peanut Butter Icing, 174
Peanut Butter Icing, Whipped,
  205
Pretzel Icing, 197

Rainbow Cookie Cake, *106*,
    107–8, *109–11*
Samoa Doughnuts, *224*,
    225–26, *227*
Scottie's Smash Cake, 120–23,
    121–22
Slutty Cake, *248*, 249–52,
    250–51, *253*
S'mores Cupcakes, 94–95,
    95–97
Sundae Cupcakes, 208, *209*
Chocolate Chip Cookie Dough
    Cupcakes, *246*, 247
    Icing, 178, *179*
    Slutty Cake, *248*, 249–52,
        250–51, *253*
    Topping, 244
Cinnamon
    Cake, 60–61
    Cheesecake Icing, 193
    Crumble, 242, *242*
    Glaze, 229
    Icing, 171
    Icing, Whipped, 205
    Peanut Butter Cheesecake
        Icing, 193
    Peanut Butter Icing, 174
    Snickerdoodle Icing, 182
Cocoa mix. *See* Hot Cocoa
Cocoa powder, for recipes, 24
Coconut
    Cake, 148–49
    Cake, The, *150*, 151
    Filling/Topping, 245
    Goo, 245
    Hummingbird Brittle, *114*, 115
    Hummingbird Cake, 112–13
    Hummingbird Cupcakes, *114*, 115
    Icing, 203
    Samoa Doughnuts, *224*,
        225–26, *227*
Coffee. *See* Espresso
Cookie Dough

Chocolate Chip, Cupcakes, *246*,
    247
Chocolate Chip, Icing, 178, *179*
Chocolate Chip, Topping, 244
Slutty Cake, *248*, 249–52,
    250–51, *253*
store-bought, for recipes, 25
Sugar, Icing, 175
Sugar, Topping, 244
Sugar, Vanilla Cake with,
    48–49, *49*
Cookies and Cream Cake, *166*, 167
Cookies and Cream Chocolate
    Icing, 176
Cookies and Cream Cupcake, 164,
    165
Cookies and Cream Icing, 176
Cooling racks, 21
Cornbread Cake, 152–53, *153*
Cream Cheese. *See also*
        Cheesecake Icing
    Chocolate Icing, 185
    Hummingbird Cupcakes, *114*,
        115
    Icing, *184*, 185
    Peanut Butter Icing, 185
    Pumpkin Spice Cake, 128, *129*
    Strawberry Cake, *54*, 55
Crumbles
    Cereal, 243, *243*
    Chocolate, 243, *243*
    Cinnamon, 242, *242*
    Funfetti, 243, *243*
    Graham Cracker, 242, *242*
    Oreo, 242, *242*
    Shortbread, 243, *243*
Cupcake liners, 20
Cupcakes
    Chocolate Chip Cookie Dough,
        246, 247
    Chocolate Sundae, 208, *209*
    Cookies and Cream, 164, *165*
    Hot Cocoa, 187, *187*

Hummingbird, *114*, 115
Peanut Butter Cup, 90, *91*
piping fillings into, 162
S'mores, 94–95, *95–97*
Vanilla, with PB&J, 46, *47*

D
Dairy, 24
Disposable plastic piping bags, 22
The Double Cookie Cake, *179–80*,
    181
Doughnut Cake, 66–67
Doughnut Icing, 170
Doughnut Icing, Whipped, 205
Doughnuts
    Cake, *220*, 221
    Samoa, *224*, 225–26, *227*
Drizzle, chocolate, making, 259
Dulce de Leche
    Cake, 82–83
    Icing, 183
    Icing, Whipped, 206
    making your own, 83

E
Eggs, for recipes, 24
Electric stand mixer, 19
Equipment and tools, 19–22
Espresso
    Chocolate Cake, Grandma
        Annie's, 98
    Chocolate Crumble Cake, 99,
        100–101, *102–3*
    Chocolate Icing, 177
    Coffee Cake, 88
    Coffee Caramel Icing, 191
    Glaze, 229
    Icing, 177
    Icing, Whipped, 205
    Pumpkin Spice Latte Cake, 128,
        129

Espresso (*cont.*)
  Pumpkin Spice Latte Icing, 200, *201*
  Whipped Pumpkin Spice Latte Icing, 206

F

Fillings
  Coconut, 245
  piping into cupcakes, 162
Fine-mesh sieve, 22
Flour, for recipes, 24
Food coloring, 24
Food processor, 19
Freezers, uses for, 22
Fruity Pebbles cereal
  Cake Doughnuts, *220, 221*
  Cereal Cake, 79
  The Cereal Cake, *80*, 81
  Cereal Crumble, 243, *243*
  Cereal Icing, 196
Funfetti Cake, 78
Funfetti Crumble, 243, *243*

G

Glazes
  Caramel, 236
  Chocolate, 222, *223*
  Cinnamon, 229
  Espresso, 229
  Hot Cocoa, 231
  Lemon, 228
  Maple, 235
  Marshmallow Fluff, 232, *233*
  Matcha, *234*, 235
  Peanut Butter I, *90*, 237
  Peanut Butter II, 237
  Pumpkin Spice, 230
  recipe yields, 217
  Salted Caramel, 236

Strawberry, 228
Vanilla, 218, *219*
Graham cracker pieces
  Graham Cracker Crumble, 242, *242*
  S'mores Cupcakes, 94–95, *95–97*
Green tea powder. *See* Matcha

H

Hot cocoa (mix)
  Cake (basic), 68–69
  Cake (decorated), *70*, 71–72, *73–77*
  Cupcakes, 187, *187*
  Glaze, 231
  Icing, 186, *187*
  Icing, Whipped, 207
Hummingbird Brittle, *114*, 115
Hummingbird Cake, 112–13
Hummingbird Cupcakes, *114*, 115

I

Ice Cream Sandwiches with Pancake Cake, 146, *147*
Icings
  Brownie Batter, 202
  Cake Batter, 199
  Cereal, 196
  Cheesecake, 192
  Chocolate, 168, *169*
  Chocolate Cheesecake, 193
  Chocolate Chip Cookie Dough, 178, *179*
  Chocolate Cookies and Cream, 176
  Chocolate Cream Cheese, 185
  Chocolate Espresso, 177
  Chocolate Pretzel, 197
  Cinnamon, 171
  Cinnamon Cheesecake, 193

Coconut, 203
Coffee Caramel, 191
Cookies and Cream, 176
Cream Cheese, *184*, 185
Doughnut, 170
Dulce de Leche, 183
Espresso, 177
Hot Cocoa, 186, *187*
Lemon, 173
Maple, 189
Marshmallow, 190
Matcha, 188
Neapolitan swirl, creating, 162, *163*
Nutella, 190
Peanut Butter, 174
Peanut Butter Cheesecake, 193
Peanut Butter Chocolate, 174
Peanut Butter Cinnamon, 174
Peanut Butter Cinnamon Cheesecake, 193
Peanut Butter Cream Cheese, 185
Pretzel, 197
Pumpkin Spice, 200, *201*
Pumpkin Spice Latte, 200, *201*
Real Mint (Nana Icing), 198
recipe yields, 159
Salted Caramel, 183
Snickerdoodle, 182
Strawberry, 172
Strawberry Cheesecake, 193
Sugar Cookie Dough, 175
Vanilla, *160*, 161
Icings, Whipped
  Chocolate, 204
  Chocolate Peanut Butter, 205
  Cinnamon, 205
  Doughnut, 205
  Dulce de Leche, 206
  Espresso, 205

Hot Cocoa, 207
Lemon, 206
Maple, 206
Matcha, 206
Nutella, 204
Peanut Butter, 205
Pumpkin Spice, 205
Pumpkin Spice Latte, 206
Salted Caramel, 207
Vanilla, 204

J

Jams and jellies
  Rainbow Cookie Cake, *106*,
    107–8, *109–11*
  for recipes, 25
  Vanilla Cupcake with PB&J,
    46, *47*

K

Knives, 21

L

Latex gloves, 21–22
Lemon
  Cake, 56
  Glaze, 228
  Icing, 173
  Icing, Whipped, 206
  Limonana Cake, 57, *57*

M

Maple
  Glaze, 235
  Icing, 189
  Icing, Whipped, 206
Marshmallow Fluff
  Cookies and Cream Cake, *166*,
    167

Glaze, 232, *233*
Hot Cocoa Cake, *70*, 71–72,
  73–77
Hot Cocoa Cupcakes, 187, *187*
Marshmallow Icing, 190
for recipes, 25
S'mores Cupcakes, 94–95,
  95–97
Marshmallows
  Hot Cocoa Cake, *70*, 71–72,
    73–77
  Hot Cocoa Cupcakes, 187, *187*
  S'mores Cupcakes, 94–95,
    95–97
Matcha
  Cake, 84
  Cakes, 85, *86–87*
  Glaze, *234*, 235
  Icing, 188
  Icing, Whipped, 206
Measuring cups and spoons, 19
Milk, for recipes, 24, 25
Mint
  Icing, Real (Nana Icing), 198
  Leaf Cake, 155
  Limonana Cake, 57, *57*
Muffins, Everything But the
  Kitchen Sink, *134*, 135
Munchie Brittle
  Dark Chocolate, 262
  White Chocolate, 262

N

Nonpareils
  Banana Cake with Peanut
    Butter, *136*, 137–38,
    139–40
  Cake Doughnuts, *220*, 221
  Chocolate Chip Cookie Dough
    Cupcakes, *246*, 247
  Chocolate Espresso Crumble
    Cake, 99, 100–101, *102–3*

Chocolate Sundae Cupcakes,
  208, *209*
Classic Birthday Cake, 169, *169*
Pumpkin Spice Cake, 128, *129*
Pumpkin Spice Latte Cake, 128,
  129
Rainbow Cookie Cake, *106*,
  107–8, *109–11*
for recipes, 24
Scottie's Smash Cake, 120–23,
  121–22
Slutty Cake, *248*, 249–52,
  250–51, *253*
Nutella
  Icing, 190
  Icing, Whipped, 204
  Mini Banana Cake Loaves,
    132–33, *132–33*
  for recipes, 25
Nuts. *See* Almond; Pecans;
  Walnuts

O

Offset spatulas, 22
Oreo cookies
  Cake Doughnuts, *220*, 221
  Cookies and Cream Cake, *166*,
    167
  Cookies and Cream Icing, 176
  The Double Cookie Cake,
    179–80, 181
  Oreo Crumble, 242, *242*
  Slutty Cake, *248*, 249–52,
    250–51, *253*
Oven mitts, 20

P

Pancake Cake, 144–45
Pancake Cake, Ice Cream
  Sandwiches with, 146, *147*
Parchment paper, 20

Pastry brush, 21
Peanut Butter
    Banana Cake with, *136*, 137–38,
        139–40
    buying, for recipes, 25
    Cake, 116–17
    Cheesecake Icing, 193
    Chocolate Cake, *90*, 91
    Chocolate Icing, 174
    Chocolate Icing, Whipped, 205
    Cinnamon Cheesecake Icing, 193
    Cinnamon Icing, 174
    Cream Cheese Icing, 185
    Cup Cupcakes, *90*, 91
    Glaze I, *90*, 237
    Glaze II, 237
    Icing, 174
    Icing, Whipped, 205
    Mini Banana Cake Loaves,
        132–33, *132–33*
    Scottie's Smash Cake, 120–23,
        121–22
    Vanilla Cupcake with PB&J,
        46, *47*
Pecans
    Hummingbird Brittle, *114*, 115
    Hummingbird Cake, 112–13
    Hummingbird Cupcakes, *114*, 115
Pineapple
    Hummingbird Cake, 112–13
    Hummingbird Cupcakes, *114*, 115
Piping bags, 22
Piping tips, 22
Plastic wrap, 21
Potato chips
    Dark Chocolate Munchie
        Brittle, 262
    White Chocolate Munchie
        Brittle, 262
Pretzel(s)
    Chocolate Icing, 197
    Dark Chocolate Munchie
        Brittle, 262

    Icing, 197
    White Chocolate Munchie
        Brittle, 262
Pumpkin Spice
    Cake (basic), 126–27
    Cake (decorated), 128, *129*
    Glaze, 230
    Icing, 200, *201*
    Icing, Whipped, 205
    Latte Cake (basic), 127
    Latte Cake (decorated), 128, *129*
    Latte Icing, 200, *201*
    Latte Icing, Whipped, 206

Q

Quinoa, puffed
    Dark or White Chocolate
        Crunch, 263, *263*

R

Rainbow Cookie Cake, *106*, 107–8,
    109–11
Red Velvet Cake, 154
Round cake cutters, 21
Rubber spatulas, 19
Rulers, 21

S

Salt, for recipes, 24
Salted Caramel Glaze, 236
Salted Caramel Icing, 183
Salted Caramel Icing, Whipped, 207
Samoa Doughnuts, *224*, 225–26,
    227
Sanding sugar
    Cake Doughnuts, *220*, 221
    Limonana Cake, 57, *57*
    for recipes, 24
    Vanilla Cake with Sugar Cookie
        Dough, 48–49, *49*

Scissors, 21
Scottie's Smash Cake, 120–23,
    121–22
Sheet pans, 20
Shortbread Crumble, 243, *243*
Sifter, 22
Skewers, 22
Slutty Cake, *248*, 249–52,
    250–51, 253
S'mores Cupcakes, 94–95, *95–97*
Snickerdoodle Icing, 182
Spatulas, offset, 22
Spatulas, rubber, 19
Sprinkles
    Banana Cake with Peanut
        Butter, *136*, 137–38, *139–40*
    Cake Doughnuts, *220*, 221
    Chocolate Espresso Crumble
        Cake, 99, 100–101, *102–3*
    Chocolate Sundae Cupcakes,
        208, *209*
    Classic Birthday Cake, 169, *169*
    The Double Cookie Cake,
        179–80, 181
    Funfetti Cake, 78
    Funfetti Crumble, 243, *243*
    Ice Cream Sandwiches with
        Pancake Cake, 146, *147*
    Neapolitan Cake, 92, *93*
    Rainbow Cookie Cake, *106*,
        107–8, *109–11*
    for recipes, 24
    Scottie's Smash Cake, 120–23,
        121–22
    Slutty Cake, *248*, 249–52,
        250–51, 253
    The Tie-Dye Cake, *36*, 37–42
Stand mixer, 19
Storage canisters, 21
Strawberry
    Cake (basic), 52–53
    Cake (decorated), 54, *55*
    Cheesecake Icing, 193

Glaze, 228
Icing, 172
Neapolitan Cake, 92, *93*
Rainbow Cookie Cake, *106,*
   107–8, 109–11
Sugar. *See also* Sanding sugar
   Brown, Cake, 50–51
   brown, storing, 24
   for recipes, 24
Sugar Cookie Dough
   Icing, 175
   Topping, 244
   Vanilla Cake with, 48–49, *49*

T

The Tie-Dye Cake, *36, 37–42*
Tools and equipment, 19–22
Toppings
   Chocolate Chip Cookie Dough,
      244
   Coconut, 245
   Coconut Goo, 245
   Crumbles, 242–43, *242–43*
   Dark Chocolate Munchie
      Brittle, 262

Dark or White Chocolate
   Crunch, 263, *263*
Hummingbird Brittle, *114,* 115
making brittle, 255
Sugar Cookie Dough, 244
White Chocolate Munchie
   Brittle, 262
Towels, 20
Turntable, cake, 21

V

Vanilla
   Berry Cake, *210, 211, 212–13*
   Cake, Classic, 34–35
   Cake with Sugar Cookie Dough,
      48–49, *49*
   Chocolate Chip Cookie Dough
      Cupcakes, *246,* 247
   Classic Birthday Cake, 169, *169*
   Cupcake with PB&J, 46, *47*
   extract, for recipes, 24
   Glaze, 218, *219*
   Icing, *160,* 161
   Icing, Whipped, 204
   Neapolitan Cake, 92, *93*

Samoa Doughnuts, *224,*
   225–26, 227
Slutty Cake, *248, 249–52,*
   250–51, 253
The Tie-Dye Cake, *36, 37–42*

W

Waffles, made from cake batter, 29
Walnuts
   Carrot Cake, 142–43
   Chocolate Chip Carrot Cake,
      143
   Everything But the Kitchen Sink
      Muffins, *134,* 135
   Mini Banana Cake Loaves,
      132–33, *132–33*
Wax paper, 20
White Chocolate
   Crunch, 263, *263*
   Hummingbird Brittle, *114,* 115
   Munchie Brittle, 262
Wire cooling racks, 21

NOTES

Hope you love your cakes as much as I do! And remember, life is what you bake it.

😉 ♥

Melissa